At the Heart of the Matter

A *Spiritual Journey for Caregivers*

Dr. Eboni Ivory Green

WESTBOW
PRESS
A DIVISION OF THOMAS NELSON

Scripture taken from the King James Version of the Bible.

WestBow Press books may be ordered through booksellers or by contacting:

WestBow Press
A Division of Thomas Nelson
1663 Liberty Drive
Bloomington, IN 47403
www.westbowpress.com
1-(866) 928-1240

ISBN: 978-1-4497-1596-0 (sc)
ISBN: 978-1-4497-1597-7 (dj)
ISBN: 978-1-4497-1595-3 (e)

Library of Congress Control Number: 2011928526

Printed in the United States of America

WestBow Press rev. date: 05/06/2011

This book is dedicated to the memory of my grandmother Frankie Q. Roberts, the wind beneath my wings.

Contents

Foreword:
Today My Heart Cried

Today my heart cried.
Not a small cry, but an open up the levy and let the floodwaters
of Noah cry, a forty days and forty nights cry.
I opened my heart and cried, not a small cry for those who judge,
instead of walking them to the light, instead of holding the
hands of those who are lost at all costs, to show us the way.
I opened my heart and today I cried for families of
those with empty hearts and wounded souls.
I opened my heart and today I cried and flooded the floodgates with
tears; there was an empty feeling, one that I could not identify.
I opened my heart and today I cried because "crying is one
of the healthiest things you can do" (Bob Deits).[1]
I cried because "I almost never cry, but lately I cry all the
time, and I think it helps" (Lance Armstrong).[2]
Today I cried and understood the reason why I needed to cry and allowed
my true feelings to shine through the sadness, and the tears flowed.
I opened my heart and today I cried for the great sense
of loss I presently feel. I cried because "those that sow
in tears shall reap rejoicing" (Psalm 126:5).
I cried because "the soul would have no rainbow had
the eyes no tears" (John Vance Cheny).[3]
I opened my heart and today I cried, and it felt so good to cry.
It was the best cry I've ever had.

—Dr. Eboni Green

YOU SEE, YESTERDAY THE WORLD lost a great spirit, and our heavenly
father invited an unforgettable soul into His kingdom. Loss is a frequent
conversational topic among caregivers. Although over the years I have

experienced a great many losses, no loss has felt as immense as the recent loss of my grandmother.

Before I began writing this book, my grandmother came to visit. When she said she was coming, all I could do was think about the list of things I had to do coupled with the fact that my brother-in-law, sister-in-law, and niece were already staying in our home. Feeling overwhelmed and overloaded, I found a quiet place (which was hard to find in our full home) and cried. I just wasn't sure how I could fit another person in my home or another task in my already booked schedule. After shedding a few tears, I pulled myself together, took a deep breath, and looked to find something positive in the situation.

I was trying to be open to teachable moments—those times when we are implored to learn a life lesson. You see, God molds each of us into what He wishes us to be, and He always supplies us with teachable moments. Teachable moments are either missed opportunities for personal growth or learned life lessons that fill our basket of experiences. In an effort to be open to God's teachable moments and seek the hidden blessings, I welcomed my grandmother into my home with open arms.

By the third day of my grandmother's visit, I knew, and so did she, why we needed this special time together. We had not had an opportunity to become friends. We had a strong foundation as grandmother and granddaughter, but we lacked the time to sit down and get to know each other personally and as adults. My childhood memories of her were of a strong-willed, multitasking mother, grandmother, nurse, and missionary. She confirmed that she, too, had an outdated perception of me.

It pleased me to add my grandmother to my list of friends. At seventy-eight years old, she still had much to give me. On her visit she also gave those in my inner circle and my home peace where chaos once resided. By the conclusion of her visit, I truly understood her long-lasting commitment to ensure my happiness. Her visit afforded a reciprocal relationship where I was finally able to offer her something after she had given so much to everyone all her life.

Had she not come to visit, look at all the blessings that would have been missed and the many teachable moments and life lessons I would have lost.

J. H. Jowett[4] fully expressed my feelings about losing my grandmother when he stated, "The ability of God is beyond our prayers, beyond our largest prayers! I have been thinking of some of the petitions that have been entered into my supplication innumerable times. For what have I asked? I asked for a cupful, and the ocean remains! I asked for a sunbeam, and the sun abides! My best asking falls immeasurably short of my Father's giving, it is beyond that anything we can ask."

I would never have thought to ask for a better understanding of and relationship with my grandmother, but God knows what we need before we know. E. H. Chaplain[5] confirmed this assumption when he said, "out of suffering have emerged the strongest souls; the most massive characters are seared with scars." Without feeling the pain of loss and having the scars to prove it, lessons may be forgotten. Jack Wintz[6] explained in *Making Sense out of Suffering*, "as humans, we will never make total sense out of the mystery of suffering. But we cope with it most sensibly by participating as actively as we can in the healing process, and by entrusting ourselves to the supreme source of love and wisdom." My grandmother's legacy is understanding, learning, and recognizing what God has to offer. I pray that with continued growth, I will understand the meaning of life. Let us pray together that you, too, find what it all means.

Acknowledgments

I would like to extend warm and heartfelt thanks to my loving and supportive husband, Terrence. Thank you for your help with editing and for being my sounding board and partner. Thank you for giving up your dreams to pursue our dreams together.

Thank you to my four little ones, Asia, Tre', Jordan, and Terryn, for your unconditional love and the lessons I've learned from being your mother.

To my mom, Debra, thank you for your support, your love, and your friendship. Thank you for all the hugs and honesty and for being such a wonderful mother.

To my dad, Jose, and mom, Laura, you are my angels. Thank you for the long hours at the table working on geometry, the support during my teens, and all the love through the years. Thank you for believing in me when I did not believe in myself. I am blessed to have you in my corner.

To Gemes and Doris, thank you for sharing your spiritual gifts and helping Terrence and I understand our ministry.

To my sister Shayna and my cousins, Cynthia and Doresa, you know what your love and support mean to me.

To my extended family Ella Mae, Emma, Johnny, Matt, Nikki, David, and Marie Perry, thank you for loving and accepting me.

Thanks to all of my supporters who were not mentioned by name.

Of greater importance, thank you, God, for the opportunity to experience such a spiritual awakening.

Introduction:
At the Heart of the Matter, There Is Good

At the heart of the matter . . .

. . . there is good in all things, when by appearances life is cloaked in
gloomy, somber, and doleful emotions expressed through free-flowing tears.
. . . there is good during seemingly endless, sleepless, restless nights.
. . . there is benevolence which exists wherever
there is opportunity for progression.
. . . there is good especially when patience and humility are
exhibited through our interactions with our fellow man.
. . . there is good, especially when we observe all
that is pleasing to the heart and soul.
. . . everything becomes graciously translucent and tremendously colorful.
. . . there is something commendable expressed in thoughts
and ideas, exhibited through trust in God.
. . . I know there is good, because at the heart of the matter there is you.

—Dr. Eboni Green

FOR SOME TIME NOW, I have wanted to write something that would
motivate caregivers because those caring for others inspire me in a
way I am unable to fully express. Henri J. M. Nouwen[7] came close to
expressing my true feelings related to caregivers when he explained
that "the one who cares makes it clear that whatever happens in the
external world, being present to each other is what really matters. In
fact, it matters more than pain, illness or even death."

Each day, while working with those in our communities who
compassionately and selflessly provide care to others, some connection
is made that gives me comfort, reason, mission, and purpose in life.

1

As Octavia E. Butler[8] stated, "every story I write adds to me a little, changes me a little, forces me to re-examine an attitude or belief, causes me to research and learn, helps me to understand people and grow. . . . Every story I create creates me. I write to create myself."

I agree with Octavia Butler in that the writing process creates me, and so I dedicate this spiritual journey to those caring for and about others. The chapters in this book are designed to guide you in this journey. Our journey will involve a minimum of three things: commitment, an open mind, and most important, you. I think if we are going to grow spiritually and move toward making changes in our lives, we must be open to developing a deeper understanding as to who we truly are, as a part of our mission to the service of others.

The very definition[9] of *journey* uses the word *travel* and puts me in mind of a really extravagant adventure. In the adventure, I see a caravan of people traveling together. This "caring" caravan includes health professionals, our families, and those in our communities who support and care with us through this adventure.

We can think of the principle of time as we transform the way we care for ourselves as well as others. We can take time to really brainstorm with our loved ones to find the best possible solutions for our caregiving situation.

On this journey we should allow ourselves the freedom to explore solutions that have yet to be executed. Remember that when we are dealing with personal relationships involving the heart, there is no quick fix. Stephen Covey[10] confirmed this idea in his book *Principle-Centered Leadership* when he stated, "There is no quick fix, where you can just move in and make everything right with a positive mental attitude and a bunch of success formulas."

We must honor ourselves with the truthfulness that accompanies any journey involving the spirit. Every suggestion may not work in its entirety. The beauty of this journey resides in uniqueness and the potential for self-assessment and personal growth. In other words, take the meat and throw away the bones. Use what applies and discard the rest. When we explore making changes at the heart of the matter, we are seeking opportunities to make lasting alterations in the way we view our very important roles.

Caregiving is a twenty-four-seven experience. There is no time clock tabulating our hours, and the whistle does not blow at the end of our eight-hour shift. Through this journey we call caregiving, we are prompted to search for the meaning in our mission of service to others.

As we begin this journey, we must ask ourselves some questions. What are we being compelled to learn through experiences and teachable moments? Moreover, what are we being compelled to learn through the calling to care and the mission to serve others?

This book is meant to move us into deeper levels of reflection on our mission to care. We must open our hearts and give ourselves permission to seek healing to be transformed into more compassionate beings. As James E. Miller[11] stated, "However you choose to express yourself know that you are encouraging your own healing by doing what you do. You are finding ways to accept, bit by bit, the reality of what it all means." Let us pray to find meaning in our spiritual journey.

Points to Ponder

Please take a moment to address the following questions as you begin this journey.

1. What are your goals as they relate to caregiving? Please list one to three caregiving goals.

    _____

    _____

    _____

    _____

2. What you wish to learn about others on this journey?

    _____

    _____

    _____

    _____

3. What you are being compelled to learn about yourself, and more specifically, about your mission to the service of others?

    _____

    _____

    _____

    _____

4. What events contributed to helping you recognize your calling as a caregiver?

    _____

    _____

    _____

    _____

Famous Quote

It is your face that you see reflected in the water and it is your own self you see in your heart.

—Proverbs 27:19

ONE
Creating a New Consciousness

The Winds of Time, the Winds of Change

The winds of time change with the tides that drift in from the sea,
just as the transitions of life flow continuously.
The transitions of life represent opportunities for growth,
missed opportunities and opportunities taken.
The trials of change and the winds of time express knowledge
and understanding that we are not the first nor will we
be the last to experience the transitions of life.
The winds of time transform perceptions, propelling the
current drifting on the momentum of the winds of time,
equivalent to riptides that roar onto the ocean's seashores.
Sometimes the waves roll in softly.
Occasionally the waves come pouring in swiftly, whipping the sea's shore.
When sitting by the seashore, we see life's transitions, and if we
are quiet, we can hear the wisdom of the seashells of life,
expressing the confusion felt during transitions.
If we are perceptive and open to life's lessons, potential growth is limitless.
The winds of time are constant on the course of living, loving, and learning.
Continuously changing
hence, now, and forevermore.

—Dr. Eboni Green

RECENTLY I HAD A CONVERSATION with a gentleman, now caring for his wife of fifty years. He openly discussed the many changes in his marriage following his wife's diagnosis of Alzheimer's disease. He began by sharing that she no longer remembers him and often searches for parents who have long passed. He has cherished their relationship thus far; however, he is in the process of creating a new consciousness; that is, he is making changes in the traditional way he viewed their relationship in an effort to continue being a husband to his wife. Creating a new consciousness as a caregiver means partnering with those we care for to combine and work collaboratively for the good of the two. Our perceptions and responses shape everything in our world. His alteration in perspectives allows him to cope with the physical, emotional, and social results of the disease process. The simple act of taking a step back enabled him to transform and open himself to his newly defined role, which changes daily. He transformed the way he responds to the circumstances in which he and his wife found themselves as a result of Alzheimer's disease. Although she may not always remember who she is, she does feel the love radiating from and being lavished on her by her husband.

The Caregiver's Journey[12] explains the root definition of what it means to care for another. Toft, Pohl, and Kay state that caregiving means "admitting we don't always have the answers or know what to do. It means admitting our fears, taking time for ourselves and getting help when we need it." Caregiving also means gaining a deeper understanding of our loved ones as well as ourselves, to make pertinent changes to grow together.

The act of making small, gradual, paced changes can offer motivation during difficult relationship transitions. Douglas Pagels[13] provided an excellent example of transformation in the following statement:

> The older I get, the more aware I become of the ebb and flow of certain feelings in my life. I know for instance, to save certain things for the times when my inner strength is like a steady wind—filling the sails to take me where I need to go. Some tasks ask me to wait for a better day, until I've got plenty of energy to get where I'm going, or wait until my confidence is growing stronger. I may delay a difficult call that must be made, a visit that requires my full happiest face, or a duty that demands an abundance of courage. If I can wait until the time is right, I find I'd more likely get to my destination. In the same way that you can't sail out to sea when the tide is out, you

need to heed the ebb and flow of the feelings in your life. Like waves on the ocean, coming ever closer to the shore, courage and strength will rejoin you—soon, steady, and forevermore.

Douglas Pagels's words offer suggested venues to acknowledge personal/caregiver-related strengths through opening ourselves to the opportunities that exist in our present circumstances. We can gain a greater sense of who we are, a new and conscious being with enough courage to love and accept our loved ones and ourselves just as we are. By opening our hearts and minds to possibilities, we can transform even the most challenging of circumstances.

Points to Ponder

1. How do you keep an open mind in challenging circumstances?

_____

_____

_____

_____

2. What practices do you use to make sure you do not get stuck in a rut?

_____

_____

_____

_____

3. What about caregiving has transformed your relationships with your loved ones?

_____

_____

_____

_____

Famous Quote

It is not necessarily the strongest of the species that survives, nor the most intelligent: it is the one that is adaptive to change.

—Charles Darwin

TWO

Turbulence

The Roller Coaster Called Life

The roller coaster called life has constructed peaks and valleys,
with thrills that frequently overwhelm and tracks that represent
teeth that engage, connect, and hook one to another.
The teeth tracks ensure continued movement through compelled progression.
Life's lessons occur during the rapid advancement of the roller coaster,
which moves swiftly until the ride comes to an abrupt end.
The ride is rigged to run routinely, starting and ending at the same point.
No matter how routine the loading of passengers is for the
conductor, the experience is unique for each passenger.
Each cart fills quickly as passengers scurry to brace for the thrilling ride.
Some do all they can to make it to the ride, lagging behind,
and continuously return to the back of the line.
Others stand in line and come to terms with the
fact that they will never board the ride.
No matter how we get to the amusement park, we are
compelled to face the challenge of the roller coaster ride.
Sometimes the ride goes too fast, but we have little control
over the roller coaster's overpowering speed.
Sometimes the ride crawls dreadfully slow as though it will never end.
In less than sixty seconds, the ride is a thing of the past.
The wait, the sacrifice, the fear matter not, for it is the thrill of the ride that
matters, enjoying the curves, the turns with our mouths hanging open
while our eyes widen and occasionally shut in sheer fear and delight.
Our faces are flushed, our hearts pounding fast.
We ride the roller coaster trying to make the ride last.
It is the thrill of the ride that keeps us coming back.
Hot sunny days with the rain sometimes bursting
through the clouds momentarily.
Our lives are somewhat the same.
The long waits to get on the ride, representing where we want to be.
Going to such highs and lows all on one ride.
Waiting for it to begin,
sad when it quickly ends,
just like the roller coaster of life.

—Dr. Eboni Green

WHEN CARING FOR OTHERS, OUR emotions are frequently governed by the wishes and desires of our loved ones. Additionally, a majority of our relationships involve observing someone who was once vigorous suddenly or progressively losing his or her independence. Often our roles are compounded with fatigue and pressure, coupled with periods of exhaustion that combine to form a valley. It can be difficult not to take low periods personally. We should not, however, allow circumstances to hinder our collective progress. Sometimes what we consider a low point is truly an opportunity for personal and spiritual growth. Valleys often compel us to slow down and evaluate present circumstances. Dr. Richard Carlson[14] described life challenges (i.e., valleys) as road bumps. In his book *Don't Sweat the Small Stuff*, he explained that "depending on how you approach and deal with the bump, it can be a miserable, uncomfortable, debilitating experience, or it can simply be a temporary slow-down—no big deal." As individuals who care for others, experiencing life's highs and lows is normal. It is our reaction to the turbulent ups and downs that transforms life's strides.

We must persevere and reapproach the challenge of caring for those we love, especially when times are difficult. We should continuously adapt to suit the current challenges as a caregiver, keeping in mind that the care we provide may increase and our loved ones may grow worse. This means trying as many approaches to the same problems as many times as possible to make it work. Douglas Pagels[15] stated, "Your life can be what you want it to be. . . . You'll make it through whatever comes along. Within you are so many answers. Understand, have courage, be strong." Pagels's words lend wisdom to the daily challenges we face as caregivers.

We should be patient with ourselves as well as with others, giving ourselves the flexibility to react however we choose. Remember that it is our experiences that contribute to whom we are today and whom we will become in the future.

Some days we experience more peaks than valleys. Caregiving can equate to coasting on the peak of love for those for whom we care.

Fond memories of life's peaks can assist in sustaining and reinforcing our roles. Coasting on the memories of tremendous peaks may enable us to stay motivated. Furthermore, using the momentum from the high periods can act as a positive reinforcement, and times of decreased momentum can encourage us to slow down and take a break.

One of the most beautiful stories I've ever heard came from a gentleman caring for his wife of twenty plus years. The two shared a love of music. For many years it had been their connecting point, and no matter what, the two would go dancing. In time, the gentleman's wife suffered from a debilitating stroke. As time passed, the two didn't dance but continued to share a fondness for music, often sitting and listening to the radio for hours together. One day, while listening to their favorite "oldies but goodies" station, the mood and music struck the pair. The gentleman gently swept his wife off her feet, held her hand in his, and embraced her in his loving arms. Although she was unable to dance, they closed their eyes, and in that instant, their kitchen was transformed into a ballroom and the two were ballroom dancers! How romantic and loving, and what a memory on which to coast. I wept when he shared his story.

It is during difficult circumstances that true gifts shine through, explode on the forefront, and bring humanity to light. With illumination from the light of humanity, we are able to appreciate fully the aspects of our current circular caregiving relationships. When the circle of caregiving is complete, we can encounter stillness and peace amid the obstacles we face in caring one for another.

Point to Ponder

Please take a moment to address the following question:

1. Try documenting a fond memory shared between you and your loved one. When you reach a low point, you can reflect on the memory and use it for support.

_____

_____

_____

_____

Famous Quote

As you live, believe in life! Always human beings will live and progress to a greater, broader and fuller life. The only possible death is to lose belief in this truth simply because the great end comes, slowly, because time is long.

—W. E. B. Dubois

THREE

Faith

✧ × × × × × × × × × × × × × × × × × × ×

Seeing Is Believing

It can't be seen or touched.
It is frequently perceived as out of reach.
Faith's moral principles reign supreme.
It is within our grasp to sustain and fill our cup if we would only believe.
Faith is a gift.
Faith is within our power to grasp and take hold.
Without faith we miss out on God's eternal blessings.
Depend on faith.
Trust faith.
Faith fades if we do not have trust.
When life tests our faith,
We should not waver,
We should not flounder;
Instead we should stand on faith with the stillness faith requires.
Trust faith with an open heart to life lessons,
Keep in mind that God loves a cheerful heart.
So we must open ourselves to life's lessons.
Have faith, be strong.

—Dr. Eboni Green

WHAT IS FAITH? I'M SURE if we were to stop one hundred people on the street, each person's response would vary greatly. *Faith*[16] is defined as a "firm belief or trust and recognition of spiritual realities and moral principles as supreme." *Faith* is a word that is often used in a religious or spiritual context to describe a belief and trust in God, giving one the ability to be committed to something. Bickel and Jantz[17] find that "faith is not an emotion. It is objective trust placed in a very real God." Faith is a partnership that requires action on the part of the believer. Without action, faith is squandered for belief. Yet belief is just one component of true faith. It is an expressed acceptance exhibited outwardly through interactions where compassion is lavished on those we adore. Although it cannot be proven by scientific measures, the ability to maintain faith in hard times, caring times, and times of selflessness can be a sustaining force. Faith moves mountains.

Recently I spoke with a close friend who'd woken in a panic, thinking about what would happen to her family if she were not around to care for them.

In an earlier conversation with my husband, he shared the same sense of urgency when he asked, "What does faith equate to?" As we discussed his feelings, he made a profound statement in relation to faith. He said, "Faith equals self-actualization."

Faith = Self-Actualization

Faith	Self-Actualization
Is expressed in deep-seated appreciation for what we possess today and the possibilities of what tomorrow holds.	Is doing what we are called to do. When we are self-actualized, inner peace is possible.

His statement immediately connected with a discussion I have with nursing assistant students when I am teaching. When I am teaching, we often explore Maslow's[18] hierarchy of needs is a principle on which many nursing interventions are based. Maslow's theory explores the premise that basic human needs are hierarchal in nature. He further finds that one need must be met to reach the next, just like building blocks. Maslow's needs include the following:

Maslow's Hierarchy as it Relates to Caregiving

Physiological Needs

These include activities of daily living, which are needs met through eating a balanced meal, water, elimination, and so on. These are basic needs with which we assist our loved ones daily such as dressing, grooming, and knowing we will be there to assist with personal needs when the time comes.

The Need to Feel Safe

These comprise the need for a home, protection from storms, and knowing that the bills are paid. Whether care is being provided in the home setting, assisted living setting, or nursing home, safety needs include knowing that insurance, Medicaid, or Medicare is there to pay for the care we need and that we won't wake up one morning without someone to care for us.

The Need to be Loved and to Belong

These include the love and affection we seek from the closeness we find in relationships and feeling as though we are part of a family and the inner connections we feel with those for whom we love and care.

Spirituality

These include the need to seek spiritual relationships. The act of adding meaning to our lives and the lives of those for whom we care.

Self-actualization

This is knowing that you are doing the right thing at the right time as someone who cares for and about others.

Through the discussion, we try to make the connection between what we are able to provide and what someone who is being fully cared for needs. When caring for someone, we begin by meeting only the most basic physiological needs. For us to be effective, our loved ones must have the ability to depend on us to provide for even their most basic needs.

Many caregivers understand the power of spirituality and further depend on faith to sustain themselves. Some days, belief in ourselves and knowing we can do a good job caring for our loved ones is the best for which we can hope. C. S. Lewis[19] found that "relying on God has to begin every day as if nothing had yet been done." We are often awaiting the start of a new day with a chance to clear the slate and begin again. We are seeking positive interactions with our loved ones to stay motivated and confirm that we are on the correct path. We expect we can make new and different choices and gain wisdom about the importance of living each day one at a time. We have the opportunity to make a difference in our lives and the lives of others with whom we make connections. It does, however, take courage to reach for the stars and wisdom to follow through and attain our goals. As Harold Cook[20] stated, "success is finishing what God gave you to do." Finishing what God gave us to do takes faith. Reaching the point of true understanding and trust, our faith in God equals self-actualization.

In a world of time, money, and morale crunches, it becomes increasingly important to stand on faith. We can say for certain that people who have faith in something larger than themselves tend to deal with life's stresses better than those who don't. With structured faith, there is little that cannot be achieved. Having confidence in our inner strength will provide the faith needed to make it through whatever comes along. We all have moments when we feel discouraged and down. We feel overworked, underappreciated, like life just isn't going our way. We may have times when we ask ourselves, "Why me?" If we aren't careful, our faith can be shaken. Our true sense of faith has the power to sustain us across even the toughest terrain. Robert Schuller[21] admonishes, "Be hopeful, for tomorrow has never happened before." Schuller's words assist us in understanding the importance of our faith. Faith equates to knowing and believing that our families will be protected. No matter how crazy our world gets or how full we book our schedules, our faith will continue to sustain us. With faith, we understand that tomorrow may not be a better day, but the new day brings hope and the prospect of starting again with a clean slate. St. Frances Sales[22] found that "the same everlasting Father who cares for you today will take care of you tomorrow and every day. Either He will shield you from suffering, or He will give you unfailing strength to bear it. Be at peace and put aside all anxious thoughts and imaginations." Have faith, be strong.

Point to Ponder

1. What has caregiving taught you about your faith?

_____

_____

_____

_____

Famous Quote

Faith is raising the sail of our little boat until it is caught up in the soft winds above and picks up speed.

—Ralph W. Ward Jr.

FOUR
Maximizing Inner Strengths

Strength internal,
Strengths concealed,
Required before long to illuminate.
Challenges of caring magnify talents suppressed subconsciously.
Kindness,
Compassion,
Patience and understanding encompass the art of caring
and the true gift of caregiving.
We should not suppress
The important contributions only we can make in the universe.
More important, please do not overlook
the spiritual essence in each of us that is caring.
Instead we should maximize the strengths within!

—Dr. Eboni Green

WE ARE BORN POSSESSING UNIQUE gifts and talents. Life experiences compound, thereby magnifying once hidden inner strengths. Positive attributes are inner strengths standing on the sidelines, saying, "Here I am, notice me." If we want to be effective in our caring, we must maximize the strengths we possess. Maximizing our inner strengths often begins by opening our consciousness to our talents. In doing so, we unleash our souls to complete the mission that is caregiving.

Caregivers, in the practice of maximizing inner strengths, can be described as "highly functioning." Highly functioning caregivers reinvent themselves daily depending on the circumstances. Resourceful and unconventional in nature, they seek opportunities to exhibit flexibility and steer away from inflexible roles, exploring the world of caring in similar fashion to a child exploring the world.

Children share a sense of openness and leniency often suppressed in adulthood. As I have watched my two-year-old son explore the world, I have become aware of how many completely new things he tries in a day. He openly investigates the world around him through touch, sight, taste, and listening. He is not deterred if he tries something and it does not work. Instead he quickly moves to his next exploration, not taking mistakes personally. He asks for help, or rather demands it. Sometimes he stands back to observe, only to have the task mastered by the second or third attempt. As caregivers, I wish absorbing shock waves was this simple. It behooves us to turn our backs on outdated patterns offering little or no return on investment. In doing so, we give ourselves permission to emulate the leniency of children, learning from our mistakes and seeing the world from a different perspective.

With renewed perspective, it is possible to explore life and view it as an adventure. In this adventure we are often using an assumed caregiving map that must be validated. One never knows what will be encountered in the unchartered wilderness. Over time, as changes occur, we will need to reevaluate our plans and desired outcomes by surveying our caregiving course. If we desire a road map that is reflective of maximizing our inner strengths, we must make a conscious effort not to focus too much attention on where we wish to end up. Concentrating on where we wish to end up often causes close things to appear far away. Instead we should focus our attention on our inner strengths!

A friend of mine is a full-time caregiver of thirty-five plus years and is extremely busy. He still finds time to volunteer, mentoring underprivileged high school–aged children, taking special interest in students in need of extra attention, and so on. One particular student he was mentoring was down on himself and did not see possibilities for his future. This is where my friend stepped in and became a true mentor. He found a computerized career assessment and took time to sit with the young man and assist him through the assessment. Not until the two took this career assessment did they realize the multitudinous positive attributes and career choices available to the young man!

Please take this opportunity to assess the inner strengths you possess in relation to your caring role. The following assessment was designed as a tool to assess areas of strength as a caregiver.

Assessment of inner strengths

Please answer each question openly and honestly. Assign two points if you agree with the statement, one point if you somewhat agree, and do not assign any points if you do not agree with the statement. Total your points for each section. Once you have completed the questionnaire, compare your scores to identify your top three areas, which represent your inner strengths.

Section A

I tend to remain calm during a crisis.

Being with others rejuvenates me.

When things do not go as planned, this is my time to shine.

When someone asks for assistance, I am usually the first to help.

I am good at organizing things that are not organized.

Section B

I enjoy working with my hands.

Being in nature rejuvenates me.

I enjoy working outdoors.

I don't mind mowing the lawn or shoveling snow.

I take pride in seeing a project through from beginning to end.

Section C

I don't mind doing heavy housework.

I don't mind doing light housework.

I enjoy working with my hands.

I don't mind doing laundry.

I am good at organizing things that are not easily organized.

Section D

I like being a driver on a road trip.

When my family travels, I make plans for the road trip.

When my family travels in town, I like to drive. I enjoy driving.

I usually provide transportation to appointments and shopping, or if I don't presently, I wouldn't mind doing so.

Section E

I am process oriented and prefer working with tasks.

I enjoy working with numbers.

I have no problem handling financial matters, for example, balancing a checkbook or paying bills on time.

I like managing money.

I am good at balancing financials to cover household expenses.

Section F

I enjoy cooking a good and nutritious meal.

I am an economical grocery shopper.

I don't mind grocery shopping.

Others frequently say they enjoy the meals I prepare.

Cooking helps to reduce my stress.

Section G

I am able to understand complicated matters.

I can explain complicated matters to others. I have a general understanding of legal matters. I do not presently have an understanding of legal matters but would be willing to learn. I have little problem following strict guidelines.

Section H

I am good at organizing things that may not be organized.

I am able to assist with medications and prescriptions.

I can organize medications that may not be organized for daily use.

I can assist my loved one with taking his or her medication.
I don't mind researching (with the doctor or pharmacist) to find out uses, side effects, and possible drug interactions.

Section I
I am people oriented.
I do not mind performing personal cares.
I don't mind assisting someone with getting in and out of bed.
I don't mind assisting with bathing or dressing.
I don't mind assisting with toileting activities.

There are a total of 10 points possible for each section. Please take your top three scores as your caregiving-related inner strengths. The questions are not limited to those in the role of primary caregiver. To the contrary, anyone in the role of caregiver may take this questionnaire. Once you have answered the questions, discuss together one another's strengths. Assist each other to compensate for your least favorite caregiving tasks by focusing on what you can accomplish collectively. We can collaborate with others possessing strengths different from ours. Anything is possible with the power of two working together.

Interpreting Your Score

Section A: Crisis Management
If you scored highest in this section, an inner strength may be crisis management. During times when action is required, you are at your best.
Section B: Yard Management
Your inner strength may be assisting with the care of the lawn during summer and winter months, or if you are unable to perform these tasks yourself, perhaps you could locate resources to assist in this area.
Section C: Housework
Your inner strengths may be assisting with household chores or cleaning and assisting with organizing the home.

Section D: Transportation

If you scored highest in this area, you may be the person to call on for assistance with transportation. You may want to decide if you will be in charge of all the transportation for your loved one or if you will be responsible for only certain aspects of transportation. Will you do all the transporting, or will someone share the responsibility?

Section E: Financial Management

This can be one of the most important aspects of providing care in any setting. This area includes balancing the household budget and making sure that there is enough funding to cover all expenses as well as planning for future needs. This particular aspect may also involve locating and applying for insurance plans and making sure that there is adequate life insurance and supplemental insurance.

Section F: Meal Preparation

Nutritional needs are vitally important in caring for another. You may wish to involve yourself in planning meals, talking with the dietitian about the nutritional needs of your loved one, or making meals that can be frozen and placed in the microwave for later use—an alternative to making a fresh-cooked meal every day.

Section G: Legal Matters

Legal matters can be very complicated because there is so much to know, depending on the circumstances. You may wish to assist in talking with a lawyer about legal matters and relay any information back to the family for input. You may wish to go to the library to research matters for yourself.

Section H: Medication Management

Medication management is another important aspect of providing safe care. Organizing and keeping records of medications your loved one takes is important.

Section I: Personal Care

Personal care is one of those areas we don't often think about until we are faced with the prospect of providing personal care. You may wish to try some type of training to prepare ahead of time for providing personal care. Preparing can boost your confidence and keep you from feeling alone when you are faced with challenges.

In summary, each person on the caregiving team should function as a supportive component, whether we are referring to professionals, neighbors, friends, or actual family members. In most cases, if we empower one another to act in a supportive function, we increase the longevity and functionality of the caring team.

Points to Ponder

1. Try listing as many positive things about yourself as you possibly can. Include as many things as you can think of that you do well. When you have a really difficult day, try pulling out your list. Your list is designed to remind you about your positive attributes. The beauty of inner strengths is that they are evolutionary. If you cannot identify all of them right now, today, not to worry. Put away the list and pull it out when there is something to be added.

   _____

   _____

   _____

   _____

2. You do not have to wait for others to tell you that you are doing something positive. When teaching, I always ask each student to stop whatever he or she is doing and to pat another student on the back. We are not patting each other on the back for what we have done; rather we are patting each other on the back for what we will do every day without so much as a second thought. Please take a moment to pat yourself on the back.

   _____

   _____

   _____

   _____

Famous Quote

Learn to get in touch with silence within yourself and know that everything in this life has a purpose. There are no mistakes, no coincidences; all events are blessings given to us to learn from.

—Elizabeth Kubler-Ross

FIVE

Asking for What You Want

I Ask Because I Care

I ask because I care,
And I don't want to assume;
my assumptions are frequently incorrect.
When I think she's old and frail,
these are not her thoughts.
I assume she needs my help, is dependent for assistance,
Can't make it without continuous supervision,
these are not her thoughts.
When I feel the roles have reversed,
She knows nothing has changed but the pace at which she runs the race.
When I am thinking it must be done yet today,
She knows what you do not finish will be waiting tomorrow.
When I believe I have found a cure,
I am saying something new,
I know more today than yesterday,
My perceptions must be correct,
Assume I know what is best,
She thinks, "I sure wish she would ask me."
Indeed we should leave perceptions to fortune-tellers,
Instead assume nothing,
Clarify everything and
give ourselves and others permission to ask for what we want and need.

—Dr. Eboni Green

I WONDER WHETHER A THORNY bush and a beautiful flower each has roots. Roots are the true intentions determining plant type, size, color, and shape. Plants with comparable roots have potential for similar outcomes if properly soiled, sheltered, and watered. Asking for our heart's desire is like nurturing our roots.

Unfortunately knowledge is not telepathically transferred from one person to another. Circumventing the desires within is only a temporary solution suppressing authentic thoughts and desires. Whatever our heart is asking cannot be entirely suppressed; hints of our desires are bound to surface. When we know how we want something, where we want it, and when we want it, then we should say so.

The likelihood of retrieving our desires is greatly increased by the way we state requests. Making our requests known opens us to the experience of caring and can propel us toward the greatest sense of whom we are. It is on this basis that we can begin to accept that which we have always been. Doe Lang[23] stated, "Change your communication style and you can change your life. Practice is the key. When you increase mastery of communications, your confidence everywhere soars."

A recent conversation with a full-time caregiver perfectly illustrates the importance of asking for what you want. As the caregiver to a husband with Parkinson's disease, some days were better than others. However, the disease had not yet progressed to the point where he was unable to take part in his own care. Over time she began taking on additional roles, and her stress levels increased. Although assistance was available, her husband insisted they not accept it. Instead the pair tried brainstorming other workable solutions. For months her life revolved around how to talk to her husband about her increased duties and stress. Over time she became resentful and burdened. After much thought she decided it would be less stressful for her if she tried one of two things: (1) requesting the assistance of her husband or (2) hiring someone to help.

Granted this was not an easy discussion for either of the two. However, what worked for her was stating how it would help *her* if she had some assistance. She explained how assistance would increase her capacity, longevity, and overall satisfaction. Sometimes if a loved one knows how important something is to us, he or she will at least give it an honest try.

This is not always the case, however, so we should not become discouraged if the response is no the first time. Instead we should open ourselves to the possibilities of the conversation. Maybe there are points we have not thought about or vice versa.

Sometimes positioning responses away from "me" and "I" and pointing back to the overall caring goals can assist. Examples include the following: "By doing ——, we are able to keep you home longer"; "Doing —— will make it easier to care for the two of us"; "Doing —— will allow us to spend time together"; "If we do not have to do ——, it will reduce our stress and make us feel better about our situation."

The following is a confirmation, a promise, and a commitment we can make to ourselves when we need to ask for something.

> *Today I make this promise to myself:*
> *I will not suppress requests in my heart.*
> *Instead I give myself permission to ask*
> *For the things I want,*
> *Things that will make my mission to*
> *care less stressful.*
> *I affirm my openness.*
> *I affirm my willingness*
> *To make my request known.*

When I teach in the nursing assistant program, my students and I often discuss allowing clients to reach their highest levels of functioning. Allowing our loved ones or clients to reach their highest levels of functioning means that we should assume nothing and ask everything. During the two-and-a-half-week training, we reassert this principle at least one hundred times. Well, after one class in particular, the students returned for a follow-up meeting. A student shared a story about a client for whom she'd cared. She explained she'd done everything for her client over the course of the day. She'd given him a bed bath, assisted with two meals, and answered the call light at least a half dozen times during her shift. Toward the end of the day, she happened to walk by the room and noticed the client sitting up in bed. To her surprise, he was not only sitting up in bed but also performing stretching exercises.

She was overwhelmed when she saw how much her client was able to do for himself after she'd provided so much personal care. When I asked the former student, "What was your client's diagnosis?" she explained he was a paraplegic. She further explained that she did not ask if he could aid in his care before she assumed he couldn't. How do we know what another needs or wants if we do not take time to ask? We must ask for what we need as well as create an environment for others to share the same freedom.

We must create an environment to authenticate the true wants and desires of those we love and care about. We are never helping someone if we do not allow him or her to assist in his or her personal care. When we ask, we are really assisting the person for whom we care to maintain his or her independence for as long as possible. We are also assisting ourselves by only performing tasks we really need to perform. This act alone frees our time to do things we want to do.

Imagine the surprise of the caregiver when she saw her client sitting up in bed. If she'd only asked him what he had the ability to assist with, she could have conserved some energy and used it to assist other clients. Instead she spent much of her time and energy doing things her client had the full capacity to do himself.

Asking for what we want is a gift both to ourselves and those we love. Making our requests known allows us to nurture who we are and allows others to express their compassion and appreciation. We must give ourselves permission to ask for our soul desires.

Points to Ponder

1. Are you in the practice of asking for what you want?

_____

_____

_____

_____

2. Do you allow others to ask for what they want without reproach or retribution? If you do not, what steps can you take to change?

_____

_____

_____

_____

3. What can you do to allow those for whom you care to become partners in their care?

_____

_____

_____

_____

4. If you are in the habit of doing everything, what can you do to change that behavior to allow both of you to become true partners in care?

_____

_____

_____

_____

Famous Quote

Power only means the ability to have control over your life. Power implies choice.

—author unknown

SIX

Expressing Ourselves through Assertiveness

Grant Me the Wisdom to Say What I Mean

Grant me the wisdom to say what I mean now
that you need me as I once needed you.
Your need for my support helps me to understand the standard plea
that sometimes goes unmet, unspoken, and without mention.
Lord grant me the wisdom to say what I mean.
Occasionally I am unable to openly express my
feelings mixed in a mass of confusion.
Feelings deep on the inside waiting to explode to the forefront.
Needing to tell you that which cannot be expressed verbally.
Lord grant me the wisdom to say what I mean.
Frequently remaining silent, not uttering a word about my true intentions.
Shielding others from what I know they cannot handle,
for there is no true way to empathize with my current circumstance.
Divine spirit, grant me the wisdom to say what I mean.
I keep emotions bottled until they gush like a rip tide,
destroying the Hoover Dam.
So I ask for affirmation through this prayer.
I pray to say tactfully what must be said.
Lord grant me the wisdom to say what I mean:
Give me the voice and the courage to speak my mind.
Show me the light and allow its radiance to
shine through into spoken words.
Divine spirit, grant me the wisdom to say what I mean,
Grant me the thoughts and allow the words to flow
and the heart that allows all feelings to be abundantly felt.
Give me the ability to listen to the true meaning behind the words of others.
Lord grant me the wisdom to say what I mean:
And for this I am grateful!

—Dr. Eboni Green

In the movies, points are made with a mastery of language. Even if one is less assertive than another, once a scene has been set in a well-written screenplay, we are able to derive a clear picture of each character's perspective. Unfortunately, real life does not work this way: we do not have skilled writers sitting on the sidelines scripting our dialogues. There are proven principles, however, that may assist us in streamlining our communication styles to become more effective. Explore the following suggested principles for effective caregiver–care recipient communication.

What is the intended outcome of your communication?

When circumstances are already strained, we should minimize heavy topics. Instead we plan for conversations where heavy matters need to be discussed. Often we don't know how to state important messages tactfully. Sometimes we must practice our monologue before relaying a message to the intended party. A wise man[24] once said, you don't have to say everything you think. Ancient writings tell us our lips and teeth should act as "gates" controlling whatever flows out. We should explore the intended outcomes (what are you asking for?) before beginning a discussion, especially when important matters are to be discussed.

Are we sending mixed messages?

Do we say one thing and then do something contrary to what we say? For example, we might say, "Sure, I don't mind doing it" or "I don't need any help, I can do it alone," but on the inside we are thinking, "Yes, I need some help" or "No, I can't do it alone." In the long run we are not doing ourselves any favors by suppressing our needs. Maybe if we think about saying what we mean in terms of helping others, the barriers of actually "asking for what we need" can be lifted. This means allowing others to help us even when the goal is to help them. We should say what we mean when it comes to asking for and accepting help.

Are there opportunities for two-way communication?

Are we in the habit of making all the decisions, or do we (caregiver–care receiver) involve others in making decisions regarding care? Two-way communication equates to using another as a sounding board, thus keeping the lines of communication open. Open communication lends opportunities for collaborative caregiving. If we do not wish to wake up in charge of all care responsibilities, we should allow others opportunities for input through open communication.

Do we let everything pile up before talking about things?

We definitely do not want to hold our emotions in waiting until we are so angry that our communication is no longer effective. Holding feelings in can be one of the fastest ways to make ourselves ill and keep us on edge. When we have concerns, we should give others the opportunity to address them one at a time. It can be counterproductive to pile everything up as if the information is intended to be part of a soon-to-be-prosecuted criminal case. If we are the prosecuting attorney, the only option is for our loved one to act in his or her defense. As partners in care, the true intention is never to be on opposing sides; on the contrary, our ultimate goal is to work harmoniously.

Are we specific about our wants, needs, and desires?

Saying what we mean and meaning what we say is not easy, especially when one has had a habit of suppressing true feelings. Often these feelings are suppressed in an effort to cope with the trials of life. Many are afraid to say what they want, and that's why they don't get what they want. Expectations often vary greatly. It is in this gray area where disagreements may occur. It is not necessarily that someone is doing something to upset us on purpose. If we are not specific with our intentions and desires, we leave it to the interpretation of others. Certain things in life are important enough to say exactly what we want, when we want it and where we want it. When we are this specific, there is little room for misinterpretation.

Do we use paraphrasing to clarify our points of conversation?

We should make sure everything is clear when concluding a conversation. This is especially important for those very important matters often discussed in the course of caregiving. Taking an extra minute to rephrase what is being said and to clarify any gray areas can greatly assist in effective communication. Clarifying means paraphrasing or restating what was previously said in the form of a question, for example, "So what you are saying is ——" or "What I hear you saying is ——. Is that correct?"

Are we really listening to our loved ones?

I recently had a conversation with a caregiver that focused on some challenging situations she and her husband were facing together. Her husband was diagnosed as a paraplegic following a surgical procedure. Directly following the diagnosis, he became very depressed and expressed the desire to die. Each morning his wife would wake him up and greet him with "Hello, honey, good morning." And each morning he would respond, "Kill me, I want to die." For many months the two went through this ritual. After much time had passed with the same question and a similar response, his wife replied, "It's OK. If you want to die, I will even assist you. I will take you over to the hill where there is a busy intersection, and when we get there I will push you over the hill into traffic. I will do this for you, but there is one thing I want you to do for me. We paid a lot of money for your wheelchair, so when you get to the bottom of the hill, before you are hit by a car, jump out of the wheelchair. I need to sell it when you are gone." Once she responded in this fashion, he never again asked her to kill him. He really didn't want to die. What he wanted was for her to listen to him. We should ask ourselves if we are truly listening to the thoughts and feelings of our loved ones. We should always make an honest attempt to try listening to the meaning behind what our loved ones are saying.

Do we prepare for really difficult conversations?

My mother is a lawyer, and growing up, she would inevitably encounter opinions she found disagreeable. In her line of work her paycheck is basically as good as her presentation skills. To present really well, you have to practice. She found an excellent place to practice her presentations. In this space she could say anything she wanted, argue her points, and make comments about the opposing side that would not be acceptable in the courtroom. Frequently, I would walk past the bathroom and hear a complete argument focused on agreeing with or opposing something of great legal importance. Yes, I said the bathroom. Her practice courtroom was the bathroom. She would take long showers and practice her arguments. I used to be really amused by this practice. As time went on, I realized how valuable the bathroom arguments really were. What a great way to get things off your chest without having to be polished. When we are caring for others, it can be downright stressful. It is tremendously important that during stressful times we don't say anything we may regret later. Practicing our presentations, especially on really important matters, can be one of the most important communication tactics we utilize.

Do you prepare your message according to the audience?

We should prepare our messages according to the audience (are we talking to our brothers and sisters or doctors and lawyers?). Just as it wouldn't be appropriate to give a speech on calculus to a classroom full of second graders, it is not appropriate to relay information to our loved ones in medical or legal terms they can't or won't understand. Presentation really is everything. We should take all aspects of presenting into account when we are preparing to communicate with our loved ones.

Do we allow ourselves time to vent frustrations?

Whenever possible we should express our feelings either through venting privately or discussing the matter. We do not want to hold our emotions in and wait until we are too angry to reason. We can try talking to a friend, a counselor, or support group members. This way, we are able to vent but do not have to worry about ever hearing our frustrations repeated. As hard as it may be initially, we should allow ourselves to feel whatever we wish to feel. We must give ourselves permission to do whatever will make our situation better. Over time it will be better for our personal care as well as the care we provide to those we love.

Communication is one of the most important practices involved in caring for another. We can greatly decrease our longevity if there is not effective, respected two-way communication. It is a proven fact that many do not stop providing care to a loved one because of increased physical demand. On the contrary, social and emotional factors often lead to burnout. If we begin the relationship with clear expectations and keep the lines of communication open, our chances for successful caring relationships are greatly enhanced.

Points to Ponder

1. Do you suppress feelings and then explode when you have reached your limit? If the answer is yes, what can you do to change this practice?

   _____

   _____

   _____

   _____

2. Do you allow your teeth to act as gates or do you say whatever comes to mind? What practices might be employed to decrease ineffective communication?

   _____

   _____

   _____

   _____

3. What are the results of your present communication practices? If you are not getting the desired outcome, what can you do to change?

   _____

   _____

   _____

   _____

Famous Quote

I don't know the key to success, but the key to failure is trying to please everybody.

—Bill Cosby

Suggested Exercise

You can write out a list of behaviors you would like to change about your communication. Start off changing one thing at a time. Review the list and check off the changes as you or others notice them. Try going back to the list in six months and again in one year to reevaluate progress. You can do this until you have reached your communication goals. Then maybe there will be new goals or additional practices on which you would like to work.

SEVEN

When Life Happens, Bounce Back with Resiliency

Forever Resilient...

Through the trials of others, I understand my experiences are minimal.
Through the lessons taught by others, I understand
I do not have all the answers.
Through the pains of others, I understand the pain
I have experienced cannot measure.
Through the burdens of others, I understand my load is not that heavy.
Through the financial hardships of others, I understand
profitability and successes are eternal.
Through the search for material possessions such as
larger homes, I understand home is in the heart.
Through the mistakes and blunders of others,
I understand how human we are.
Through the love expressed by others, I understand
the Divine's presence in every man.
Through trials and lessons,
Through pain and burdens,
Through the search for financial success and material growth,
Through blunders and mistakes,
I promise to remain resilient.

—Dr. Eboni Green

EIGHT

Reaping Your Harvest

I have planted seeds and I want to harvest
seeds of prosperity and great deeds.
Seeds planted in rich soil with nutrients from the
care provided to those I love dearly.
I have planted seeds and I wish to harvest a positive crop, in all its luster,
with trunks and bushes thick, vibrant and full of life.
I've planted good seeds and I'm ready to reap my harvest.

—Dr. Eboni Green

I THINK I SUPPRESSED OR forgot about the day I was driving on a dark highway. My daughter was in the car with me—she was maybe four months old and crying loudly in the backseat. I was very young at the time and definitely not an experienced driver. In my haste to meet her needs, I turned to the backseat to give her a bottle. My eyes were only diverted for what seemed to be seconds, but when I turned back around, the car was dragging against the viaduct. In that instant I wrecked the car and found myself within feet of a raging riverbank. Had I been thinking, I would have pulled over to the side of the road, but I didn't, and in the end the car had the dents to prove it. I do not believe there was some terrible force at work dragging the car against the viaduct. The dented car was a direct result of taking my eyes off the road. Sometimes we do this in caring for another. With good intentions we get battered and bruised, whether it is emotionally, physically, or spiritually. If we take our eyes off the road, even for a minute, we can put out negative vibes and end up making our circumstances worse.

When starting to write this chapter, I began thinking of the numerous ways to tactfully express the age-old saying "You reap what you sow." In other words, if we are planting lilies, we should not end up with a palm tree and vice versa. We must understand there is no getting around the unspoken natural laws of life because this natural balance has stood the test of time. We can find comfort in knowing that if we are caring individuals, eventually the positive energy we put into the universe is returned.

Although the existence of a natural order/golden rule is no secret, there are those intent on not observing them. Some prefer continuing to do the same things over and over even though they are not getting the results desired.

I think it would be proper to say that "life is constantly happening." Life can either happen to us or it can happen for us. When life is happening to us, we are minimally participating in the creation of our own destiny. However, the results are quite different when we choose to participate in positively shaping our lives.

Much of what we are doing as caregivers, unlike the car situation, is not within our control or the control of our loved ones, for example, illnesses our loved ones suffer or declines in functional capacity. However, there are things that are within our control, for instance, our attitudes about the world around us. If we are looking out for what is in our best interest collectively and gleaning from life what we need to grow and find fulfillment, we should have little time for distractions. We shouldn't take our eyes off the goals we have set. When life happens, we can stand with confidence and reap the seeds of our harvest.

Points to Ponder

1. Please describe your attitude about the world around you.

---

2. Research presently indicates that we understand little about how the brain works. This is a positive with respect to mind over matter. Why not try thinking at least one positive thought per hour? You can try writing down some of those positive thoughts to reflect on later.

Famous Quote

Your actions are simultaneously the result of past karma and the creation of new karma. Action creates desire. Desire produces further action. Which continues the cycle of karma. To be aware of this reality and to master your actions are the keys to creating the karma of happiness.

—Taro Gold, *Open Your Mind: A Little Book of Eastern Wisdom*[25]

NINE

Keeping an Open Mind

Description of an open mind...

Where there is an open mind, endless possibilities exist.
For a mind open to new ideas, it matters not how a task is accomplished,
so long as it is performed in love and with care.
Unclosed minds are tolerant, progressive,
unrestricted and flexible in nature.
Even the most challenging situations offer motivation and cause for a smile,
which massage the heart and soul.

—Dr. Eboni Green

HAVE YOU EVER ATTENDED A meeting (at school, church, or work) at which someone shared a great idea and, before that person could complete his or her suggestions, another reminded the group that the idea had been tried before? The group may have continued by discussing the reason why the idea did not work. In this situation, we are forced to take one side or another, looking to find reasons why the idea will or will not work. Once we become defensive by taking sides, the principles of keeping an open mind go right out the window. Usually, when we take an idea or concern to another, we are not seeking a concrete answer; what we truly seek is an open mind combined with an open ear. Keeping an open mind means not getting bogged down by limitations and expectations for what life will be like; on the contrary, an open mind commits us to being flexible and open to trying something new.

During challenging times involving caring for another, keeping an open mind can become increasingly difficult. In keeping an open mind, we must be aware of the abilities our loved ones still possess.

This practice must also be balanced with giving them the space they need to accept and cope with their illness. Our loved ones will have good days, bad days, and days when they are increasingly irritable and depressed about what the future holds. We must give our loved ones and ourselves permission to feel however we want. This is a delicate balance and will take time.

Principles of keeping an open mind

Listening without making judgment

Save judgment until all the evidence is in. Understand the principle that the case may never rest. Some of the worst people I've met have been the most judgmental, often unable to measure up to the standards they set.

Listening even when we don't agree

This may mean someone in the caregiving family has opinions that differ from ours. Perhaps, at this point, we've been doing things all alone for some time, maybe for a long period of time. Just because we disagree does not give us permission to disrespect views that differ. This means fully listening to what others are saying even when there is a possibility that we may not agree.

Trying new ideas

Don't be afraid to try something new. I recently saw a program on former president George H. W. Bush in which he took up parachuting. Every year, he and his wife try something new. What a wonderful way to live: always trying something new. We shouldn't allow ourselves to become attached to outdated practices. Instead, we can try new and innovative approaches to our partnership in care.

Taking suggestions for what they are worth

Many arguments result from a difference of opinion. A suggestion is just that: it is a suggestion as to what someone might do if he or she happened to find himself or herself in similar circumstances. We can either take the suggestion or place it on the back burner. Some suggestions are useful, whereas others don't seem logical or wouldn't fit our situation. We can take suggestions for what they are worth.

Being flexible

Remember that anything brittle breaks. Unless we want to crumble, we should stay flexible. There is an entire chapter devoted to the subject of flexibility. To reiterate: it is extremely important to remain flexible and try new approaches.

Throwing out preconceived notions

There are no written rules when it comes to caring. Much of what we do has not been done before, and if it has, it has not been done by us. There is no "normal" caregiving situation in which everything goes as planned. We do the best we can with what we've got. And you know what? That's good enough. We should do what works best for our situation when we need to do it and not make any excuses in doing so.

Keeping our minds open also equates to suspending judgment until we have all the facts. When our minds are open, we provide undivided attention for our loved ones to express and explore what they have in their hearts. Take the following into account when working toward keeping an open mind.

If we keep an open mind, we do not allow ourselves to continue ineffective practices. Instead, we plan for those things that are within our control and keep our minds open for things that are not. The key is keeping our hearts and minds open.

Sometimes friends and loved ones who are removed from providing care day-to-day may not understand how overwhelming and time consuming caregiving can be. As time progresses, there may be decreasing numbers of long-term friends standing beside us. We should keep an open mind to the possibilities that family and friends may not know what we are experiencing if we do not share our experiences with them. Once we have shared information with our family and friends, we must give them permission to do what they can to assist, and then we must accept the help.

We must allow ourselves and our loved ones to explore fully the opportunities life has to offer. We will meet low points in our roles and in our lives—it is natural. Sometimes we feel down or depressed until we understand the entire situation. If we continue to make decisions based on presumptions, we will inhibit our personal and collective growth. Keeping an open mind relates to the way in which we provide care to our loved ones as well as the personal care we provide for ourselves. This means giving ourselves permission to do whatever works best for our individual caring partnership. In doing so, we will be able to reach the goals we have set together and influence the way we feel about our very important roles.

Point to Ponder

1. Are there barriers prohibiting you from keeping an open mind? If there are, try listing a few.

_____

_____

_____

_____

Famous Quote

It's not what happens to you, but how you react to it that matters.

—Epictetus

TEN

Stillness

When you don't know what to do and it seems that all is lost, you
can stand still, embrace life's challenges, and He will be there.
When you are stuck and confused and your gas tank needs a
refill, you can stand still, be patient, and He will be there.
When all seems lost and you have nothing left to pay the cost,
you can stand still, be patient, and He will be there.
When your family and friends don't understand the pain you
presently feel, you can stand still, be patient, and He will be there.
Standing still requires faith and discipline, doing what you want
requires none, so stand still, and I guarantee He will be there.
When you are going through the trials of Job and you can't see the light at
the end of the tunnel, you can stand still, be patient, and He will be there.
Standing still and understanding His will requires trust and patience.
Doing what you think is best for you is human, requiring little or
no discipline, so stand still, be patient, and He will be there.

—Dr. Eboni Green

BEFORE WRITING THIS CHAPTER, I happened to become really ill.
During the previous two months before I became ill, we had three
major events planned, and I was teaching both day and evening
classes. We were on a mission to make sure I would have a week off
for Thanksgiving and two weeks for Christmas. As it would turn out,
we had one of our most important classes, a pilot program for family
caregivers, scheduled. But before we made it to that class, we had a
major event planned for the first week of November, a medication aide
class scheduled for the second week, and the pilot program starting the
third week. Well, I had been pushing myself for weeks and hadn't been
feeling very well, but I just kept booking my schedule. On the Sunday
night before the medication aide course was to begin, I had to rush to

the emergency room, where I was diagnosed with an ear infection. OK, fine! I thought I would rest a day or so, take some medication, and feel better all without any interruption in my teaching schedule. Not so: the more medication I took, the worse I felt. I couldn't hold anything down, couldn't sit up, couldn't do anything but be still. I decided there was no reason I shouldn't be feeling better after the second day of feeling ill, so I set an appointment with my physician. "A double ear infection," she said, "and you'll need to take the rest of the week off. Do you need me to write a note for you to have the time off work?" I didn't need a note, but it wasn't going to be easy to reschedule classes. What choice did I have? I was so sick that I couldn't do anything but be still. My husband had to go to the office and cancel the classes the next day.

Although I was forced to be still, the results were profound for my life and the lives of those around me. When we are on our backs, totally dependent on others for our care and support, it's surprising how rapidly our perspectives change. I needed a change in my perspective, just as I needed to be still.

Stillness can occur by accident. There are circumstances that happen in life which prevent us from doing things we wish to do. Often we encounter barriers because the timing is not right or because we don't need to make a certain move right now. Being still is the answer. Stillness may seem unnatural; however, when we accept the things we cannot change and decide to make the best of the situation, instead of gritting our teeth complaining about it, the results can be surprising.

There are times in our lives when it is more difficult to be patient. For example, it may be difficult to be patient when we are waiting for the birth of a baby, a family member is having surgery, or we are anxiously waiting to hear about a new job. These events are potentially life changing. Challenges are a normal part of what we do; it is our response to the challenge, however, that makes a difference, and sometimes that difference is being still and patient.

While I was lying flat on my back, nothing became clearer to me than how much focus I was placing on external issues that, in the grand scheme of things, would not give long-lasting results of a positive nature. Basically, I would not want to be remembered for being a "great housekeeper" or "boy, she sure worked a lot." But I was headed down the path of being externally focused. I was caught in the cycle of doing and not really living. Being still slowed me down from taking this particular path. During my illness, I had the opportunity to see that although the dishes weren't done and the furniture needed dusting, and even though I had to cancel classes, the world would continue moving forward. What makes a difference is the lives we touch, the people with whom we connect. It is their memories and their stories that keep us living well beyond our years. We do not have to do everything, and we certainly don't have to become ill to practice stillness. The practice of stillness should be incorporated in some form into our daily lives. We can practice stillness through yoga or silent prayer: it may be in the bathroom in the morning or late at night, where there is just a quiet place and time to be still. We are often surprised at the problems that can be solved and the possible new perspectives we have if we are able to get away mentally.

After a discussion with students about the topic of stillness, one student said that he made simple adjustments in the way he interacted with his son. Instead of going behind his two-year-old to pick up toys throughout the day, he began playing with him and instead waited until his son went to sleep to pick up the toys. This was a practice of stillness because instead of doing, he was actually learning to enjoy what was important to his two-year-old son. This he found to be much more productive.

Sometimes stillness comes in the form of doing things to revitalize ourselves: getting to know ourselves and our inner workings, better understanding what is going to make us happy. We can't help anyone else if we don't take care of ourselves. Stillness is a practice that will assist us in caring for ourselves. Try it—I'm sure the practice of stillness and self-care won't be disappointing.

Points to Ponder

1. Try listing the many ways possible to practice stillness.

_____

_____

_____

_____

Once you have a list, you can incorporate these practices one at a time into your daily routine. You can try each practice for a week, adding a new practice each week. In a matter of a few weeks, you will have incorporated self-care tips into your daily routine.

2. I couldn't find a place where I felt at peace until I created my own garden. I took my front yard, which was filled with grass, and created my personal paradise. The only thing missing is the bench I plan to add this summer. Is something or someplace physically or mentally possible that will signify peace?

_____

_____

_____

_____

Famous Quote

Part of being a winner is knowing when it's enough. Sometimes you have to give up the fight and walk away, and move on to something that's more productive.

—Donald Trump

ELEVEN

Give All He Asks and Take All He Promises

Sittin' in the Church Parking Lot . . .

There's something about just being here sittin' in the church parking lot,
although there are no church activities scheduled here today.
The sovereign silence of the church lot draws me
closer to the Divine spirit just the same.
There's something about making just the slightest or simplest
change in my surroundings that bends the ear,
The ear to hear the birds chirping the overture of the Divine.
The words of the Divine offer a fresh,
vibrant,
different
perspective.
This gives me hope.
There's something about the practice of sitting patiently,
without movement,
in silence,
with no one else present.
I'm drawn here despite the emptiness of the lot.
There's something about just being here, sittin' in
the church parking lot where the wind
blows the whispers of the Divine's sweet and tender promises.
Today in this church lot I find all that I need to carry on one day further.
Through this experience I am comforted,
knowing I am never alone.
By all accounts there's nothing profound about
sitting here in this old church lot.
With time I gain understanding,
comfort never comes from one restricted place.
So I sit here in the church lot and affirm daily
the challenges
as I carry the burdens of caregiving,
and I go to my place of refuge.

Today I find solace,
in this church parking lot,
for who knows what tomorrow holds.
With each day my place of sovereign solace is subject to change.
In fact, I never know where confirmation will be found.
Comfort, serenity, peace, stillness and calm always
find me in the midst of this caregiving storm,
When on that occasion the Divine meets me
just sittin' in the church parking lot.

—Dr. Eboni Green

RECENTLY, I RECEIVED AN E-MAIL with the title of this chapter contained in the message. At first glance, there does not seem to be an underlying message. Take a second look, however, at the title: "Give All He Asks and Take All He Promises." Seems simple enough, doesn't it? Giving all He asks and taking all He promises means accepting the gifts of others with open arms. It means doing that which God asks us to do while having enough faith and wisdom to accept that which God has in store for us. Sometimes we underestimate our contributions to the lives of others. What would the world be like without us for even a day or two? When we are suffering physically, financially, or emotionally, it becomes more difficult to enjoy what our lives have to offer. Taking care of someone suffering physically or mentally has its challenges, and some of us are caring for loved ones with a mixture of limitations. As a result, we find ourselves the link for a loved one and thereby completing one another. Shouldn't we learn to accept and work toward making the best of our lives?

We must ask ourselves if we are fully living our lives. Do you know or remember what it is like to really live, or has it been so long since you have had a good day that you cannot remember what a good day is like? When you think about a good day, you should consider the completeness of what one day has to offer. Many things begin and end in a matter of one day: we are born in the course of one day, as do we die on a certain day. We are married, have children, and sometimes even become full-time caregivers in a matter of one day. Giving all that He asks and taking all that He promises relates directly to opening your heart to what God has to offer.

Not long ago, my mother and I were talking, and she shared a story about getting to the airport. She was on her way to Omaha from California to assist in the planning of my grandmother's memorial service. Her friend offered repeatedly to give her a ride to the airport in California. At first, my mother refused, stating, "No, I don't need a ride to the airport. I can take myself or catch a cab." Her friend persisted. Still my mother declined her offer. That evening, my mother thought about it, and later, she called her friend to accept the ride to the airport. Her friend gladly drove to pick her up and was promptly there to assist her at four o'clock in the morning.

We do this all the time. We pray for help and ask for help and know we need the help. However, we often refuse a helping hand when it is offered. When we do not accept help from others, we may in fact be closing the door on blessings. We should not shut the door on our blessings. More importantly, we should not shut the door on someone else's blessings. Instead, we should give all He asks and take all He promises.

Point to Ponder

1. Are you open to accepting what God has in store for you? If not what can you do to change?

_____

_____

_____

_____

Famous Quote

All the rivers of thy grace I claim. Over every promise write my name, for this reason I kneel before the Father, from whom His whole family in heaven and on earth derives its name. I pray that out of His glorious riches He may strengthen you with power, together with all the saints, to grasp how wide and long and high and deep is the love of Christ, and to know this love that surpasses knowledge—that you may be filled to the measure of and the fullness of God.

—Ephesians 1:8–19

TWELVE

Making a Life Plan

· ◇ · ◇ · ◇ · ◇ · ◇ · ◇ · ◇ · ◇ · ◇ · ◇ · ◇ · ◇ · ◇ · ◇ · × · × · × · × · × · × · × · × · × · × · × · × ·

Without adequate planning, how will we know where
we are going? More importantly, what will tell us that
we have arrived at our desired destination?

—Dr. Eboni Green

THE SEARCH FOR BALANCE CAN be exhibited through the outcomes we strive to reach daily and are best expressed in a plan. Developing a plan for our lives as caring individuals will allow our unique qualities to shine and spill into action. A life plan can serve as a guide for both you and your loved one. We may wish to incorporate our personal values as they fit into the big picture to persist in pursuing goals as they relate to caregiving. When our loved ones are no longer with us, our plans may serve as a reflection for comfort, knowing that together, we did what was best for our situations.

To make a life plan, we should begin by determining what we wish to accomplish collectively (as caregivers and care recipients). We may even wish to write a purpose statement outlining the care we are providing for a loved one. The purpose statement could serve as a personal mission statement. Steven Covey[26] recommends that we think of a mission statement as a "personal declaration of independence." Hamel and Prahalad[27] believe that to qualify as a mission statement, any statement should take less than three minutes to explain clearly to an audience. A mission statement should serve as encouragement for those incidences when we need encouragement and revolve around our caregiving, but it is not designed to give action steps as to how to get there.

Try brainstorming, and then organize these ideas into a practical mission statement for the care that you provide to your loved one.

My Mission Statement

_____

_____

_____

_____

_____

Through the expression of a mission statement, we are transforming our thoughts. It is my opinion that continually transforming individuals open up so that they are able to adapt to challenging situations. As transformational caregivers, we understand that we do not have to generate all the ideas. We understand that every task is important and that we cannot do it alone. This is a proven fact—we know we don't even have to try. Our written mission and life plan can act as a visual aid when caring for others.

Writing the plan

Before writing the plan, consider the following questions: What outcomes are you trying to achieve? For example, do you wish to keep your loved one at home? To what lengths are you willing to go to care for him or her? Are there resources available in the community that may assist in keeping your loved one at home? If so, what are they? Is there anyone on whom you can depend to assist you in the care of your loved one such as family or friends?

Please begin by listing the outcomes you would like to see as a result of the care you are providing:

_____

_____

_____

_____

_____

What do you wish to accomplish on a daily basis? Is it enough for you just to maintain your sanity? What are your goals for personal care? Do you wish to provide the personal care? Can someone assist, or can you hire someone to perform these services? Are you trying to keep a schedule? If you are, what does your schedule look like?

Try listing what you wish to accomplish daily for your loved one:

_____

_____

_____

_____

Planning pitfalls

- Be sure not to take your role in life too seriously and, as a result, lack the capacity to change when what you are doing is not working.
- Do not forget the principle of not just doing a good job but being the best at what you do, although others will not always have your same standards.
- Have the patience or wisdom to start over again each day, with a clean slate.
- Batman had Robin, Superman had Lois Lane, Simba had Pumba and Timoné, Winnie the Pooh had an entire cast of supporters—do not forget to include others who will assist in reaching the goals in your life plan.
- Do not forget to inform others of your plan and encourage their participation.
- As resourceful as you may be, do not forget that you don't know everything.
- Just as successful organizations don't try to be everything to everyone, you shouldn't promise your loved one things you can't deliver.

- Implementing your life plan is up to you individually. Change won't begin if it does not begin with the heart.

When we defy the natural laws of transformational caring, we end up as "conditioned caregivers." Conditioned caregivers overcondition themselves to provide care for others and, in the process, forget about service to themselves. Conditioned caregivers are prone to being available without hesitation when others need assistance. We do not wish to fall into the traps that often arise because we are so conditioned to taking care of others and, in turn, lose our personal sense of direction. As a result, we may become too ill or weak from caring for everyone else, even when we know we need to care for ourselves. We must be careful not to condition ourselves so that when the phone rings or someone says we are needed, we say yes, no matter how much we have helped already. It is ludicrous for a person to think that he or she can commit to caring for others when the person cannot commit to caring for himself or herself.

To transform ourselves from conditioned caregivers to transformational caregivers, we can begin by altering our way of thinking. Transforming caregivers understand that their mission and life plan is a work in progress.

In the previous chapter, I told a story about becoming ill. Well, because I was ill, I had to cancel a course. We had ten or fifteen students registered for the course who had rearranged their work schedules to attend. For the most part, the students were fine with rescheduling; however, a couple students were extremely upset. In my two and a half years of business, I had received very little negative feedback, and so I took this very personally. One student yelled and screamed and even questioned the validity of offering classes. For a few days, I was very upset, and then I read Galatians 5:22–23, which stated, "The fruit of the spirit is love, joy, peace, longsuffering, kindness, faithfulness, gentleness, self-control. Against such there is no law." This verse encouraged me to embrace my mistakes and progress quickly to learning.

We shouldn't waste energy on what could have been. All I could do was focus on the results—the upset student—make adjustments accordingly (slow things down), and move toward my future with a slightly changed perspective. When I heard myself explaining to the student, "I'm sorry. If there was any way I could have continued the class, I would have done so. What can I do to make it up to you?" I even went so far as to apologize for getting sick, and the student's response was, "Did you ever even have a class scheduled?" I asked, "Can I send you a refund, or perhaps you would be interested in taking another class that fits your schedule? I'll even schedule one-on-one time with you so that you can finish the class. Whatever I can do, I will do." Still the student was insulting.

Throughout this unpleasant experience, I began to understand that I can't be everything to everyone and nothing to myself. I learned that I must care for me because I am the only me there is, and I learned to seek the lesson rather than looking where to place blame. Iyanla Vanzant[28] describes this focus in what she calls "Postulate Four," embracing the lesson and not focusing on the challenges. She says, "God does not punish us. We punish ourselves with guilt, shame, and fear when we choose not to act in concert with inherently divine nature." Even when we can't directly see the correlation between our present challenge and a life lesson to add to our life plan, if we look closely, I'm sure we can take something positive from almost any challenging situation.

As caregivers, we are truly "agents for worthy principles" looking to support and care for those we love. Our life plans will assist us in doing the most with our lives in our present role.

Points to Ponder

1. Are you able to speak openly about your personal feelings and share your plan with someone? If so, try naming him or her and describe what makes it so easy to talk to that person.

_____

_____

_____

_____

Food for Thought

No matter how noble our intentions, without adequate planning, we can become scattered and lose direction and focus.

—Dr. Eboni Green

Famous Quote

How you spend your time is the only true measurement of your priorities of life.

—Nancy Hunter Denney

My Life Plan as a Caring Individual

My Mission Statement:

_____

_____

_____

_____

_____

What do you wish to accomplish overall as a result of the care you provide?

_____

_____

_____

_____

Who are your supporters, and what roles can they play to assist?

_____

_____

_____

_____

What will you do to care for yourself while you care for your loved one?

_____

_____

_____

_____

Is there anything your loved one can do to assist in his or her personal care? If the answer is yes, try listing what he or she can do.

_____

_____

_____

_____

THIRTEEN

Putting Your Life Plan to Work

The most yielding of all things,
Overcomes the hardest of all things.
That where there is no crevice.
Hence I know the value of action without striving.
Few things under heaven bring more benefit
than the lesson learned from silence.
And the action taken without striving.

—*The Tao, Sacred Way*, Talbert McCaroll, editor[29]

EVERY LIFE HAS A PLAN. In the previous chapter, we developed life plans and mission statements. Naturally, the next step is to migrate our thoughts to putting our life plans to work. The key is that we have begun planning for our lives as people who care for others. More importantly, we have developed an understanding that it is better to plan rather than to launch into a life full force, only to end up in the wrong direction. Because we have just written a plan, we are ahead of the game and have taken steps vital to our personal success, the success of our loved ones, and the success of our community.

To begin executing our life plans, we should start off where we presently are. We should also make sure we are not basing our plans on the achievements of others. Rather we should base our plans on who we are by defining our long-term goals. We should keep from focusing on everything that needs to be done and focus instead on what life has to offer today. Richard Carlson[30] stated that "so much of the stress we experience has to do with our minds being too many places at the same time." We should incorporate focusing on something we enjoy and appreciate in our life plans. This time will offer time for reflection on our present strengths.

When something does not go as planned, we should learn whatever we can and move forward. We don't want to get stuck doing the same things over and over again. Vince Lombardi[31] stated, "When you're doing something wrong, doing it more intensely isn't going to help." Instead, we should take a step back and learn whatever we can from our experiences. We must remember to forgive ourselves. Forgiveness is a gift, so we should keep in mind that we cannot please all people all the time.

Begin by reviewing the plan

Begin by reviewing your plan by scanning it over to ensure that it is a complete picture of your mission and vision for your life as you care for another. Feel free to make adjustments as needed, or just review it if it is an accurate representation. Make sure action steps are included and goals are well defined. Post the plan in a place where it will be seen a couple times a day.

Before implementing your life plan, you should check the following.

Is the plan flexible?

Make sure the plan has room for adjustment in thoughts and ideas.

Will the plan maintain your interest?

Be sure the plan is worth implementing and that the steps that have been laid out will keep your interest.

How will you know when you have reached your goal?

It should be clear when you have reached your goal, and you should have a plan to celebrate successfully reaching your goal.

Are the goals well defined?

The key to achieving goals is to have them well defined. When goals are not defined, trying to meet them can keep you in a state of confusion.

If you don't know where you are going, how will you know when you get there? It's confusing just thinking about going someplace without knowing your final destination. Well-defined goals are a pertinent piece of the road map to success.

How will you reach your goals?

These are your action steps. Each action step is a detailed description that will lead directly to reaching the overall goal. You should make sure that your action steps are clear.

Who will assist you in meeting your personal goals?

Define those who plan to assist in any possible way in completing each action step. How will each person assist? What is his or her role? How often will he or she need to complete the defined action steps?

What additional skills and training will you need?

Do you have any questions for which professional services can assist? Are there courses offered in the community that would assist in meeting any of your personal or caregiving goals? There are often a wide variety of courses offered in the community, ranging from communication courses to courses that focus on the personal care of others—seek them out.

Once you have a written plan, you should evaluate the plan's overall ability to act as a working action plan. You can begin the practice of listing your accomplishments. The practice of listing accomplishments may assist with staying motivated. The use of journaling and checklists can also be effective motivational practices. Documenting progress and mapping out actions may aid in making a mental note of your accomplishments. Once you have written a plan, you must have the motivation to implement it. The following is a list of suggestions for motivational longevity to implement your plan.

We should be gentle with ourselves

We should maintain flexibility in our planning and always remain gentle with ourselves. We can pray for direction; however, we shouldn't beat ourselves if things don't go exactly as planned. Our lives are ever changing, so our plans should allow for flexibility. It is hoped that as we continue down the path of prosperous knowledge, we will understand that the best way to gain "knowledge" is through experiences. Sometimes it is during difficult times that we learn the greatest lessons. If something goes wrong, we should learn and continue to move toward our goals. Most importantly, we must be gentle with ourselves while learning and adapting our plans for life.

Celebrate successes along the way

On the occasions when we are successful in reaching our goals, no matter how incremental, we should take time out to stop and celebrate them. There can be a tendency to minimize the successes in our lives and to turn increased energy on the goals we didn't meet. Instead of focusing on unmet goals, we should try to spend more of our time and energy focusing on our successes. By no means am I suggesting that we not take mental note when we encounter opportunities to learn. What I am suggesting is to spend very little of our energy focusing on anything negative in nature. Instead of holding on to negative situations, we should learn and move on.

We should never give up but rather persist until we find a way to achieve our goals

If an action step is ineffective, we shouldn't waste time trying the same old, tired approaches. We should give ourselves permission to try different approaches until we find what works. On his show, Dr. Phil[32] frequently poses the question, "How's that working for you?" to his guest and viewers. Why continue a practice that is not getting the results we desire? This is why it is so important to maintain flexibility. When I speak of flexibility, what I am referring to is the flexibility we allow ourselves and others. Most importantly, we should never allow a brick wall to keep us from doing what we are meant to do. Keep in mind that there are many approaches to making it over any wall, and we should just keep trying until we find a way to conquer it.

Achievements can be used as building blocks for the future

Building on each achievement can enhance our potential growth. Each individual achievement represents a building block for future successes. We should be mindful of successful practices we discover and make them a natural part of our repertoire. If there is anything not working, we should discard the practice; we don't want to dwell on the ineffectiveness of any practice.

We should maintain a positive attitude

Keeping a positive attitude will assist us in moving forward. When we are thinking positive thoughts, we have little choice but to feel positive.

Once we complete our plan, we should not tuck it away for a later date. Instead, we should try posting it and incorporating small but significant changes to reach our goals.

This plan will not happen by itself. To see changes, we must take the necessary steps to continue caring for one another successfully.

Point to Ponder

1. If something does not coincide with your mission, then the answer to the request may have to be no. Learn to say no.

_____

_____

_____

_____

Famous Quote

If you want to accomplish the goals of your life, you have to begin with the spirit.

—Oprah Winfrey

FOURTEEN

Finding a Harmonious Life Rhythm

When it is quiet and still I try not to go too deep inside myself,
to the place where I am in touch with my feelings.
Frequently I wish to detach, unlock, release and unload the reality of the
situation at hand, because it is too complex to completely understand.
Keeping it real, my detachment and uncensored focus help me deal.
So, I evaluate the rhythm of life and the effects
and naturalness life's rhythms hold.
Often it's the touch of your hand that reaches my
soul and makes life's rhythms whole.
I wish to somehow give to others, without subtracting from myself.
The challenge is change.
The challenge is finding a way to support the growth of one another.
The challenge in a nutshell is finding a harmonious life rhythm.

—Dr. Eboni Green

THE PRINCIPAL FOCUS OF FINDING a harmonious life rhythm relates to seeking rhythm rather than trying to find an equal balance. The word *balance* implies that life will equal out like it does when we are balancing a checkbook. In an extreme example, this would indicate that when something positive happens, something of an equally negative nature would naturally have to occur. Of course, this in an incorrect assumption, although we sometimes must look deeply to find the greatness in seemingly negative situations. Often it is the development of patience that lends wisdom to the natural rhythms of life. We can also find our rhythm using some of the following approaches.

Providing comfort to others with our presence

We can offer silent support to those in our surroundings without forcing ourselves on anyone. Just knowing we are around to provide support can offer peace to those we love. In addition we can offer comfort to others by being present and learning to accept the comfort others bestow upon us.

Finding other passions outside of our role as caregivers

If we don't allow ourselves time away from what we do as caregivers, then we are likely to experience burnout. Most of us had interests prior to caregiving, and we should continue having interests outside our role as caregivers. We must make time for ourselves because time won't make itself. A family member whom I love dearly limited her potential by placing restrictions on herself. She decided there was no way she should start any additional projects, that is, without first cleaning three rooms in her very beautiful home. For a full year, she wouldn't get a job. She wouldn't finish the college courses she needed to complete her bachelor's degree. In truth, for a full year, she ended up stagnating her personal happiness and well-being as well as subtracting from the fullness of her life by placing these limitations on herself. We must make planning a priority and follow our plans through with action. If we do not make it a habit to schedule time for ourselves, nothing will happen.

Practicing where we are and not with problems that occur

Even when there are challenges, we are still experiencing life. We must try not to focus on what isn't going well because even in the midst of challenges, good things may happen. We should focus on what is going right in our lives as well as in our caregiving situations.

Enjoying what exists today

Whatever is going to happen will happen. If we are facing the long-term loss of a loved one, there are still small moments that happen each day that let us know we are alive. We should try to enjoy and cherish those moments.

Being selective when we choose to take on additional roles

There is a delicate process to finding a harmonious life rhythm. Often there are tasks we must swap to fit them into our already booked schedules. We should choose them carefully and prioritize accordingly in relation to level of importance.

Building a network

Those of us who don't have extended family nearby or who, unfortunately, don't get along with our own families can still build a network of friends who can help in the care of our loved ones, and some of them may even become our greatest supporters.

Not getting stuck feeling sorry for ourselves

Rachel Harris[33] found that "feeling sorry for yourself is a lot like getting caught in quick sand. In both cases a mysterious force pulls you down until you are feeling overwhelmed and helpless. Your only hope is that someone will come along and rescue you. . . . On the contrary, feeling sorry for oneself is de-energizing and often projects an image of helplessness and inadequacy." If we are not stuck feeling sorry for ourselves, we will not have to wait for someone to come to our rescue. It could be a long wait.

Finding a rhythm that works best for our individual situations will take time, patience, and persistence—it is not going to happen overnight. When I began to evaluate where I was spending the majority of my time, I came to understand why I was getting the results I was getting. Subconsciously, at some point, I made the decision to focus my energy on work. I convinced myself to work really hard now, even if it meant spending too little time with my family. As a result, my daughter's grades ended up in the toilet. She who had always been on the honor roll was now bringing in threes and fours, which equates to Cs and Ds. Her attitude toward me was horrific, and she was always miserable. My husband and household were also not receiving the care they needed. The laundry was backed up, and I hadn't cooked a meal, something I love to do, in months. My personal health was also in jeopardy because I didn't take the time to work out. My life rhythm was seriously off kilter. I had to take a serious look at where the goal of "working now and taking care of everything else later" was going to get me. What I needed was a change in focus. Continuing down the path of putting everything before my family would have been detrimental. I had to make some changes, and make them quickly. If I had continued this totally outward focus, my life rhythm may have been off forever. I needed to find a life rhythm that would allow me the freedom to work as well as play, but more importantly, to focus on what really mattered most. I knew that what mattered more than my career, without question, was my children's well-being and my marriage. My focus needed to reflect my inner beliefs.

Sometimes I get intent on finishing a project and, in the process, forget about living. I'll bet I'm not the only person in the world to lose focus. While writing my first book, I placed myself on a fast-paced writing frenzy. Mind you, no one else pushed me into the schedule; I placed the pressure on myself. I would spend so much time writing that I hardly had time to do anything else. When I started writing this spiritual journey, I decided I would not place any stipulations on how much or how often I would write. I decided that even if it took a year or more to finish, so what? What's the big rush? While writing, if my son tried to climb into my arms for a hug or wanted to watch *Monsters, Inc.* for the thousandth time, I would close the lid on the laptop. I made it a priority to start cooking a healthy dinner and began exercising. I can't say the results were immediate; however, I did start to notice differences in the way I was feeling. I could work smarter with fewer hours instead of working longer and harder. I could spend more time planning and less time cleaning up because of a lack of planning. I could spend less time sleeping and more time living. To say it plainly, I found a harmonious rhythm for my life.

When I sit back and take a look at where I was headed, I'm glad I didn't make it. I could have woken up years from now bitter with regret. Instead, I found my true self: the person, wife, mother, friend, and professional I've always wanted to be. We should ask ourselves if we are living the lives we've always wanted to live or if we are we waiting for something like the perfect job, or a certain amount of money, or some special set of circumstances before we plan to find out who we really are. Finding our life rhythm can only assist in reaching our heart's desire.

Point to Ponder

1. Is there anything in your present situation throwing your life off rhythm? If so, do you have thoughts about what can be done to change your circumstances?

_____

_____

_____

_____

Famous Quote

O God, help me to believe the truth about myself, no matter how beautiful it is.

—Marcrina Wiederkehr[34]

FIFTEEN

Don't Trade the Shoe for the Boot

Don't think of problems as difficulties. Think
of them as opportunities for action.

—author unknown

THE PHRASE "DON'T TRADE THE shoe for the boot" admonishes that we
should be thankful for what we presently possess. We should stay away
from focusing on how the situation would or should be better than it is
presently. Sometimes we don't know how good we have it until things
get worse. We should take time to appreciate our present blessings as
well as evaluate what we wish and hope. If one is intently focused on
her wishes and desires, as bright as she may be, she may lose sight of
the yellow brick road.

In *The Wizard of Oz*, Dorothy wishes to leave Kansas. She wishes
to protect her dog Toto from harm and also feels as though everyone
in her supporting cast is against her. In the beginning of the movie, no
one understands her plight, and she decides to run away. However, it
isn't until she faces challenges and meets lifelong friends along the way
that she understands and begins to appreciate what she had in Kansas.
Only after much soul searching does she understand that the power to
return home was within her control the entire time.

What if we are experiencing a situation that won't get better? Is this
what we want to end up spending the rest of our lives worrying about:
what should have been, what could have been, and what could be? Or
would we prefer to live each day to its fullest and enjoy traveling down

the twists and turns of the yellow brick road? On the yellow brick road, we have the potential to meet new friends, and learn new lessons.

Life's actions are yet visual reminders of our thoughts expressed through the decisions we make daily. Don't trade the shoe for the boot.

Points to Ponder

1. Name a circumstance that seemed worse than it really was. Now consider your reaction to the situation: was it positive or not so positive?

_____

_____

_____

_____

2. What was learned from the experience?

_____

_____

_____

3. Is there anything that could have been done differently then? Is there anything that can be done differently now?

_____

_____

_____

_____

Famous Quote

It's easy to be independent when you've got money. But to be independent when you haven't got a thing—that's the Lord's test.

—Mahalia Jackson

SIXTEEN

Continuous Self-Improvement

I Do Believe . . .

I believe—that sometimes when I'm angry, I have the right to be angry,
But that doesn't give me the right to be cruel.
I believe—that just because someone doesn't love the way you want
them to doesn't mean they don't love you with all they have.
I believe—that maturity has more to do with what types of
experiences you've had and what you've learned from them and
less to do with how many birthdays you've celebrated.
I believe—that it isn't always enough to be forgiven by others.
Sometimes you have to learn to forgive yourself.
I believe—that no matter how bad your heart is
broken, the world doesn't stop for your grief.
I believe—that our background and circumstances may have
influenced who we are, but we are responsible for who we become.
I believe—that just because two people argue
it doesn't mean they don't love each other. And just
because they don't argue, it doesn't mean they do.
I believe—that we don't have to change friends
if we understand that friends change.
I believe—that it's taking me a long time to become the person I want to be.
I believe—that you should always leave loved ones with
loving words. It may be the last time you see them.
I believe—that you can keep going long after you can't.
I believe—that we are responsible for what we do, no matter how we feel.
I believe—that sometimes the people you expect to kick you when you're
down will be the ones to help you get back up. I believe in you . . .

—author unknown

GROWING UP, I REMEMBER MANY conversations between my mother
and her sisters. The conversation would inevitably end up on the topic of
their upbringing and what it was like to be the preacher's daughter. The

discussion always included thoughts about parents who focused on the masses and missed the moments that make up a child's life. Without changing my focus, involving serenity, prayer, exercise, and stillness, I could spend my children's moments doing and have no time to really live life. This does not mean I'm still not working to touch the minds and reach the hearts of those with whom I come into contact. What it does mean is that I can see someone now and more fully understand, without having to make excuses, that it is not always the big things that matter most. It means I don't have to focus on changing or affecting the masses. The impact of connecting with just one person at a time can be the substance of life and a basis for spiritual growth. No one made these changes for me. Change occurred by shifting my focus in one area of my life, unleashing profound results.

Making these connections equated to the versatility and structure of a spider's web. As the spider begins the web, the structure is supported by the center. The spider's web is supportive, connected, and a safe place to be. It brings its owner nutrients that find the web impossible to avoid. As we branch out to build off the sturdy center core, we find the power in the connections meeting and supporting one another to enhance our lives beyond measure.

In life, we want to do nothing less than continue to build on what we already understand. However, if we walk blindly through life, there is a tendency to lose sight of our long-range plans. There are pitfalls we can avoid, thereby allowing for continuous self-improvement.

Overthinking

We should not allow ourselves to become worn out thinking about how tired we are going to be, how long things are going to take, or what someone else thinks about what we are doing.

Holding on to crazy situations

We must detach ourselves from unhealthy situations. If a situation is unhealthy, we should break away and not hold on to things having a negative impact on our situation.

Allowing ourselves to become frustrated

When we are frustrated, it only makes matters worse. We should take time away to defuse situations before they get worse. We should not do anything out of frustration; we may regret the results.

We must count on living each day satisfied with what we've accomplished so that if it were all over tomorrow, we would be satisfied with what our lives had represented. It is my belief that this level of satisfaction is almost impossible without continuous self-improvement. The great thing is that improving ourselves is contagious—others around can't help but be affected.

Points to Ponder

Consider each of these questions after each encounter you find stressful:

1. When, where, and what were important components of the stressful event?

    _____

    _____

    _____

    _____

2. How was the event handled?

    _____

    _____

    _____

    _____

3. Did you tackle the cause or the symptoms of the problems? Did you deal with the stress or situation correctly?

    _____

    _____

    _____

    _____

4. What could be done to improve the situation?

    _____

    _____

    _____

    _____

Famous Quote

It is easy to be the person you have always been, for it requires no change, no self-reflection, and no growth. It may appear that changing yourself requires giving up something. In reality, there is no need to give up anything—you must simply add to what has been.

—Taro Gold[35]

SEVENTEEN
Putting Your Foot Down

Deep inside a lonely me,
I find the resource to be free.
It has been there all along,
growing and becoming strong.
The lord, in His wisdom, has made, all with love,
and purpose determined from above.
We face each day, not knowing the plan,
just believe in the Divine as He holds our hand.
The journey is long and sometimes quite rough,
together forever makes us tough.
Now, I believe I can go on,
to complete life and beyond,
knowing each day joy and happiness waits,
around the corner and through the gate.

—author unknown

IN THE BOOK, *How to Win Friends and Influence People*, Dale Carnegie[36] refers to a story written by Mary Roberts Rineheart. The story begins with a bright, vigorous young woman who became an invalid in order to get a feeling of importance. . . . She took to her bed; and for ten years her old mother traveled to the third floor and back, carrying trays, nursing her. Then one day the old mother, weary with service, lay down and died. For some weeks, the invalid languished; then she got up, put on her clothing and resumed living again.

The mother in Mary Roberts Rinehart's story was so very devoted to her daughter that she didn't have time for herself. Instead of *putting her foot down*, she was emotionally and physically bled dry. As a result of suppressing her needs, she dies, and the care receiver goes on to live another day. Even when we feel as though our loved ones ask for more than what they need, we may end up suppressing our feelings and allowing our loved ones to depend totally on us for their care.

The phrase "putting your foot down" may sound forceful; however, the practice can have phenomenal results. Putting your foot down means taking a stand, setting limits, and yes, even saying no. Putting your foot down can be an acceptable practice to preserve yourself and decrease your risk of burning out.

You should evaluate the following when putting your foot down.

What kinds of things are confronted?

Do you wait until you have exhausted all possibilities before saying anything?

How are they confronted?

Putting your foot down does not give free reign to treat others in an inappropriate manner. To the contrary, when you put your foot down, you are letting others in on your expectations. Sharing expectations only enhances your ability to continue providing service over the long haul.

When setting limits, are win-lose tactics involved?

You do not want to end up putting your foot down on the gas and the brake at the same time. When you do, the car of life stalls. You do not have to make the circumstances unbearable for others. This means that you do not have to make putting your foot down a power play. You are not in a battle for power or correctness. More or less, you are setting limits and laying out expectations. Each person has something valid about his or her perspective.

What practices assist in defusing negative attitudes?

What are you doing to build bridges? When you must take a stand in an area, there is always common ground on which to begin. You can start off where you and others agree and move forward to the gray areas, giving a little and taking a little and only putting your foot down on important matters. If it is not something vitally important, evaluate whether it is a good idea to take a stand on the topic.

We hurt ourselves by not allowing for time to do the things we want because of guilt. When we keep others in the dark about our feelings, wants, and desires, we rob them of the opportunity to make necessary changes. We may find it difficult to set boundaries because of pressure from others or pressure we place on ourselves. Guilt only proves to be a barrier in keeping us from doing things that are vital to our longevity as caregivers. Any time there is a concern, it is best to inform the person who can make the change. I think the following letter from President Lincoln[37] best illustrates a tactful way to express ourselves when we have concerns:

Letter from Lincoln

I have placed you at the head of the army of the Potomac. Of course, I have done this upon what appears to me to be sufficient reasons, and yet I think it is best for you to know that there are some things in regard to which I am not quite satisfied with you.

I believe you to be a brave and skillful soldier, which, of course, I like. I also believe you do not mix politics with your profession, in which you're right. You have confidence in yourself, which is a valuable if not an indispensable quality.

Lincoln continues explaining his dissatisfaction with precision and tactfulness. He concludes,

Neither you nor Napoleon, if he were alive again, could get any good out of any army while such spirit prevails in it, and now beware of rashness. Beware of rashness, but with energy and sleepless vigilance go forward and give us victories.

The practice of setting limits does not mean shaming our loved ones; to the contrary, it means tactfully letting our loved ones know when we find behaviors unacceptable. In doing so, we do not make excuses for what can't or won't be done; rather we give ourselves permission to set goals and limits and to have expectations.

Points to Ponder

1. You may decrease your risk of burnout and ensure that what you do remains fun by putting your foot down. It is an accepted practice to preserve yourself by saying no sometimes.

   _____

   _____

   _____

   _____

2. You can acknowledge your humanity: "remember that we have a right to pleasure and a right to relaxation."

   _____

   _____

   _____

   _____

Famous Quote

You can't make someone else's choices; you shouldn't let someone else make yours.

—Colin Powell

EIGHTEEN

Memories Last a Lifetime

The Threads of Life

That which we need to see will become apparent if we only open our eyes.
That which we need to feel will radiate throughout
our souls, if we only open our hearts.
That which we must do will fill our days if we would strive to become aware.
That which we need to know will fill our brains if
we open ourselves to true knowledge.
That which is bound cannot truly be freed unless the shackles are
removed, for no matter how hard you try, a bound man cannot
be convinced of his freedom; true freedom is experienced.
That which is dark does not know of darkness, until
darkness is overshadowed by the light,
and light appreciates not its abundance until darkness falls.
It is the bonds that tie us together, the threads
of life that connect us one to another.

—Dr. Eboni Green

Point to Ponder

1. One's remembrance of past experiences can be either vivid or dusky. Dusky memories are frequently task oriented. These memories fade as time progresses because they are not emotionally based. In direct contrast, vivid memories are frequently emotionally based. Vivid memories can relate to the emotions we share and experiences of life. I'm not suggesting that there are no memories about tasks. What I am suggesting is that tasks don't necessarily make long-lasting memories.

_____

_____

_____

_____

Famous Quote

So we fix our eyes not on what is seen, but on what is unseen. For what is seen is temporary, but what is unseen is eternal.

—2 Corinthians 4:18

NINETEEN

Minimizing Unnecessary Circumstances: A Useful Practice to Stay Motivated

Courage

Do not pray for easy lives.
Pray to be stronger men.
Do not pray for tasks equal to your powers.
Pray for powers equal to your tasks!
Then the doing of your work shall not be a miracle,
but you shall be the miracle.

—Phillip Brooks,
U.S. Episcopal Bishop (1835–1893)

MINIMIZING SITUATIONS THAT ARE WITHIN our span of control can reduce the stress we experience. Minimizing circumstances means being conscious of our actions and the effects our actions have on our present and future existence. Expecting too much from others can potentially become a major point of stress and distraction that interferes with our goals and dreams. Feeling depleted of energy can defeat the spirit, and with a defeated spirit, we can become aggrieved. Grief is often more profound and debilitating when the major focus of one's life has been on the needs, wants, and actions of others. Caregiving can be extremely stressful, and from time to time, there are a variety of unpleasant issues. Each individual situation has its own set of circumstances. It is how we deal with the circumstances that determines our ability to stay motivated.

When I was growing up, my grandmother would always say, "Give it a year." No matter what our prayer, if it was a life decision and we were going to her for advice, we knew she was going to say, "Give it a year."

After much thought, I realized that "give it a year" was just an intangible and yet measurable way to say to give yourself time. If we never stick to anything, especially those tasks or duties we find least appealing, how will we reach our highest level of spiritual functioning? E. H. Chaplin[38] explained, "A true man never frets about his place in the world, but just slides into it by the gravitation of his nature, and swings there as easily as a star." I do believe that some situations afford the opportunity, for us to become greater spiritual beings. If we apply the knowledge that is sometimes packaged as a challenging circumstance, we will have the opportunity to embrace challenges and grow. Each of us knows when it is time to move forward in our spiritual journeys. Let us pray that we travel renewing our spirits and filling our cups.

A very wise person named caregivers "the strangers among us." How true—caregivers are often strangers, disconnected from others sharing the caregiving mission and thereby caring in secret. When one is distanced from others, isolation can begin to feel normal. Numerous caregivers offer selfless acts providing support to frail family members and expecting nothing in return. As caregivers, we often gain inner strength from the ability to remember the love and selfless gifts offered by our loved ones. Often we pick up where we left off with previous relationship histories and move forward into "that good night" (not knowing what to expect). Picking up where we've left off can be difficult when the relationship history was not positive. We may lack the important skills necessary to build a sturdy caregiving relationship when relationship bricks are cracked or missing in the caregiver foundation (i.e., negative feelings or unresolved issues). However, Leon Bloy[39] has stated that "there are places in the human heart which do not yet exist, and into them enters suffering that they may have existence." As caregivers, we understand moving forward when a loved one is in need. With each passing day, and as the caregiving situation progresses, there are many deposits and withdrawals. Our caregiving bankbook has many transactions. Sometimes there are overdrafts, while other days offer a surplus. Let us pray that our caregiving bankbooks stay balanced.

Points to Ponder

1. Try listing positive aspects of providing care for your loved one.

_____

_____

_____

_____

2. What has providing care taught you about yourself and others?

_____

_____

_____

_____

Famous Quote

Light a candle instead of cursing the darkness.

—author unknown

TWENTY
Relinquishing Control

Submit.
Let it go.
Do all you can to relinquish control.
Disclaim all trivial tasks and allow your fingers to become
liberated and your hands unobstructed to grasp and mold.
Relinquishing control offers you the true power,
giving the illusion others have won the battle.
Minute things seem enormous to those overwhelmed,
allowing diminutive things to become missed opportunities.
Capitulate,
when you can,
as much as you can, allow yourself to be free,
to do whatever your soul desires.
Give it up.
Submit.
Let it go.
Allow yourself to relinquish control.

—Dr. Eboni Green

WHEN ILLNESS TAKES OVER, CONTROL of normal life decisions is sometimes lost. Instead of planning for the future and enjoying our present lives, we begin coping with the problems related to the illness and/or illnesses our loved ones face. In an instant, our lives and the lives of our loved ones are forever changed. We often take the situation by the horns and begin caregiving.

Recently, Dr. Phil[40] had a guest on his show: she and her daughter-in-law were experiencing problems with boundaries and, as a result, their relationship was seriously suffering. The mother-in-law insisted on making what she termed "subtle suggestions" in the form of letters and articles. She would offer advice on everything from meal preparation to weight loss. As a mother, she felt she was offering constructive support; however, her relationships with her son and grandchild were negatively affected, while her relationship with her daughter-in-law was adversarial. There were no short-term or long-term benefits to the mother-in-law's need to exercise control. When she took a step back and Dr. Phil asked the famous question "How's that working for you?" she had to agree that her tactics were getting her nowhere.

In an effort to control even the smallest of circumstances, we miss out on the true experiences of life. Trying to control everything makes any problem seem like mountains of which we will never reach the crest. Our attempt to be controlling frequently makes those around us resentful.

Contrary to popular practice, we can still accomplish what needs to be accomplished without being controlling. When we refer to *control* in caregiving, the definition of the term differs slightly from the traditional definition. Control in caregiving relates to issues of personal care, paying bills, setting appointments, determining the time of day to get out of bed or the time to retire for the evening, and even how much will be portioned out for meals. However, control can present a challenge even when our intentions are sincere. Sometimes the caregiver has a predisposition to be controlling, or vice versa. It is human nature to wish to make lasting contributions to our lives and the lives of others. This does not, however, mean that we have to try to control every circumstance. In truth, our loved ones are only wishing for and expecting some level of autonomy, some active participation in shaping their destiny. When caring for someone with decreased decision-making capacity, we should try not to be overbearing; instead we should allow our loved one the autonomy to make decisions that he or she is able to make.

In my professional career, there have been instances where, in the process of caring for someone, a client asked for assistance with something that did not seem vitally important. I remember one particular incident during which a client requested a glass of water. I took the glass of water to my client, feeling accomplished and prideful. As I handed over the nice, full glass of water, my client shared his displeasure. There was surely too much water in the glass, and there was no way he could possibly drink it. On my return to the client's room, with less water in the glass, he was still displeased. In an effort to get rid of the excess water, I had inadvertently dumped out too much ice. It took several trips to the kitchen until finally, the glass of water was to the client's liking.

Time passed, and I continued thinking about the client and the glass of water. After much contemplation, I began to understand that my client's intentions were less related to me personally and more to controlling what was still within his span of control. It was not about his cup being half empty or half full, or even how much water the cup contained. What mattered was my asking how he wanted things accomplished, things that were far more personal to him than they were to me. As long as I continued to make assumptions about what he really wanted, he was forced to correct me. What changed between the second and third trips to the kitchen? Instead of making assumptions about my client's needs or wants, I started asking him exactly what he wanted. If the request was a glass of water, I would ask, "How much water would you like? Would you like ice?" I would ask as many clarifying questions as possible in response to each request. My practice became one of relinquishing control and encouraging the client to make decisions he was capable of making.

What barriers must we overcome to realize the benefits of relinquishing control? Following are some points to ponder when beginning the practice of relinquishing control.

Assess what needs to be done and learn to let go of tasks

We should take a close look at the tasks needed to fulfill our caregiving obligations. Next we can determine and list which tasks we need to complete personally and which can be delegated. We can take a diagnostic approach to determining those tasks that we really must complete ourselves. If it is a task someone else can perform, we should let go of the task. Sometimes we feel as though we are the only individual with the capability to complete certain tasks. It is only in our absence that we realize the capacity others possess. The time we went out of town for a few days, or the time we were ill, on our return, our homes were still standing. Our homes may not have been as clean as we would have cleaned them, but everyone was still there, and everything was still OK. We can't determine someone else's pace. We can only control our responses to what our loved ones consider important. We can either give them the space to flourish or overshadow their important roles by holding on to everything. When we let go and relinquish control, we empower those around us to enhance their talents and skills.

We can resist the temptation to take over if or when things go wrong

Respect and trust can be displayed by respecting our loved ones' need to successfully reach their individual goals. Dr. Carlson[41] defines *controlling* as "unhealthy attempts to manipulate the behaviors of others." He further explains that control is insisting on having things be just so to feel secure. Behaviors such as immobilization and defensiveness are often the reactions exhibited when people don't behave the way we see fit. When something does not go as planned, we should resist the temptation to take over. Instead, we can allow those around us to utilize their talents. If we are fixing all the problems, how will those we love learn resourcefulness? Remember, when we step in, we are robbing our loved ones of the opportunity for growth, so we should resist the temptation to do so.

Offer praise and constructive feedback

It is not necessary always to express differing points and opinions with our loved ones. We can silently disagree. This practice can further strengthen our relationships and assist in creating a greater sense of being on a *team* and support for one another. In *How to Win Friends and Influence People*, Dale Carnegie[42] shares the following statement by J. D. Rockefeller: "If a man's heart is rankling with discord and ill feeling toward you, you can't win him to your way of thinking with all logic in Christendom. Scolding parents and domineering bosses and husbands and nagging wives ought to realize that people do not want to change their minds. They can't be forced or driven to agree with you or me. But they may possibly be led to, if we are gentle and friendly, ever so gentle and ever so friendly." We can focus on the positive aspects of a situation. If someone is doing a good job, meeting a goal, or even making an effort, and we notice it, we should say so. Try to focus on areas where you agree rather than exerting excess energy on areas you find disagreeable. When we are supporting, we encourage our loved ones' independence and help them reach their highest level of practical functioning. It is not through criticism that we create any long-lasting changes; however, if we support one another, boy, what changes we will see.

Offer encouragement

Encouragement to reach goals is exhibited by focusing on the attempts and efforts our loved ones make, regardless of the success of the practice. A supportive environment is fundamental for success and growth and can be displayed in hundreds of ways, including through words, tone of voice, body language, or even a glance. Many supportive moments are spontaneous. Support includes space for reciprocation and allows an individual to acknowledge his or her feelings as well as explore creative solutions, especially during times of emotional and physical crisis.

We can learn to share positive feedback by giving one another a pat on the back when strides are made. We can also allow ourselves to transform our relationships to make them more efficient and supportive.

Separate the person from the problem

We can begin shifting our focus by separating the person from the problem. When we separate ourselves from the problem, stress and hard feelings can be greatly reduced. We are often not really angry at the individual but rather the circumstance. We should not allow ourselves to take it personally when our loved ones have concerns or wish to take control of things in their surroundings. The goal for our loved ones is to have some control over aspects of life that are not easily controlled. We can try thinking of creative ways to validate our loved ones' need for control without making it apparently known. We are, in essence, assisting ourselves in having some input while catering to the need of our loved ones to feel some level of autonomy.

We can create a positive, open attitude and respect feelings our loved ones express

We should state our feelings clearly and factually as well as evaluate our mutual goals together as partners who care. Through evaluation, areas of mutual agreement should become apparent, and this is a good place to start. Dale Carnegie[43] suggests, "Ask questions with which your loved one would have to agree, keep on asking questions until finally your loved one will find themselves realizing it, your loved one will find themselves embracing conclusions they would have bitterly denied a few minutes previously." Socrates called this tactic getting the "yes, yes response." In any long-term relationship, there must be some sense of mutual respect, which must be soundly based. Trust is an important component of mutual respect and is vital to the interdependent relationship between caregiver and care recipient.

Relinquishing control relates to delegating and giving complete authority to complete tasks. This means relinquishing control without overanalyzing that which is not within our span to govern. Our actions will assist our loved ones in understanding the importance of their contributions. We can let go rather than holding everything on our shoulders. We should remind ourselves that we do not have to do it all, including making all the decisions or setting all the schedules.

When we are truly practicing the principle of relinquishing control, we are sharing information that will assist our loved ones in assisting us. If we relinquish control over those decisions our loved ones can make, we are encouraging not only their independence but our personal independence as well.

Points to Ponder

1. How do you reward those who do the things you ask of them?

    _____

    _____

    _____

    _____

2. What do you do in the form of positive reinforcement to show that a job has been well done?

    _____

    _____

    _____

    _____

3. Do you punish people when they do not behave in the way you wish?

    _____

    _____

    _____

    _____

4. Do you fail to give people permission to do the right thing?

    _____

    _____

    _____

    _____

Famous Quote

By fighting you never get enough, but by yielding you get more than you expected.

—Dale Carnegie[44]

TWENTY-ONE

Filling Your Spiritual Basket

Without the love and support of one another, the spirit is not nourished and the soul withers. With the proper nutrition, the spirit becomes vibrant and the soul flourishes in the radiant rays of the Divine.

—Dr. Eboni Green

THERE ARE INSTANCES WHEN UNDETERMINED amounts of time are spent doing things of little importance. When we take time to care for those we love, at the heart of the matter, there is little time to waste on unproductive or unimportant tasks. Our focus is on providing support and care to those who matter most. Making a difference in the way we experience life for even one moment out of each day can be vitally important. I can't think of anything more important or time better spent than caring for our loved ones in our homes and communities. As caregivers, we are assisting others in reaching their maximum potential on a daily basis. If we wish to end up with positive results, over the long run, we must have personal practices to fill our spiritual baskets.

Filling our baskets is dependent on what personally relaxes, revives, and renews us individually and spiritually. A catastrophic event, such as an illness, should not have to prompt us to begin caring for ourselves. If we allow ourselves to become slaves to caregiving, then we will become controlled by the tasks we intend to provide. If I could run to the top of the tallest mountain and scream loudly, "We must take care of ourselves!" it wouldn't express the true importance of the message I am trying to relay.

We can ask ourselves if we have experienced a time when we were unable to care for ourselves. Being unable to care for ourselves can be a humbling experience, to say the least. When we are ill, we place extreme trust in others for our well-being. If becoming a care recipient is not in our direct or future plans, we'd be well advised to take steps to keep ourselves vitalized and our spiritual baskets full.

The best example to relay the importance of caring for *ourselves* is a story of a gentleman caring for his wife, who had been diagnosed with Alzheimer's disease. He was very devoted to caring for his wife and refused any outside assistance. When I received a referral to visit for a Caregiver Wellness Assessment™, it was a last resort. The referral was never able to progress to setting an appointment to visit, brainstorm, and problem solve. Because the gentleman had a doctor's appointment scheduled for his wife and had finally scheduled a doctor's appointment for himself, he asked that I call back in two weeks. It was his intention to take time for himself after his doctor's appointment. When I called back two weeks later, he'd passed away. He'd been working so intensely to keep his wife out of the long-term care facility that he'd forgotten to care for himself. After he passed away, his wife was forced to go to a long-term care facility because she had no one else to care for her. I am not telling this story as a scare tactic; it only illustrates an extreme example of the drawbacks of neglecting to care for ourselves.

The following are suggestions to help focus our attention on our personal well-being and keep our spiritual baskets full. Only by providing adequate self-care are we able to assist others. Please use the following suggestions and adapt them to your individual situation.

We should go to our doctor's appointments

When we have scheduled medical appointments, we should go to them. Sometimes this means planning ahead to make it to our appointments. We should prepare a list of any questions we may have about our medical care. Far too often, as caregivers, we do not schedule appointments for ourselves, citing being too busy or simply procrastinating. Early detection is the key to prevention. If we are missing medical appointments, we may not be able to detect medical problems early enough.

When medications are prescribed, we shouldn't stop taking them

When our physicians prescribe medication, we should take the medication as prescribed. In nursing, there is a saying that "assistive devices won't assist if they are not used." The same rings true for medications. If the medication prescription is not filled, or the medication is sitting in the medicine cabinet or a drawer, it won't help us. It is almost worse to take a medication for a period, only to quit. Instead, we should take medications as prescribed, unless there is an adverse reaction; then it would be important to contact the doctor.

We should get a good night's sleep

We must find our balance in relation to sleep by figuring out how many hours of sleep we need to function optimally. Each person requires a different amount of sleep; however, an average of eight hours is recommended. If we need sleep aids, time to unwind, or a relaxing bath to calm ourselves, we should seek these out.

We should eat a well-balanced diet

The importance of eating a well-balanced diet does not apply only to those we love. When we eat, we should take time to sit and enjoy our meals. We should try not to snack on commercial snack food; instead, we should try fresh fruit and vegetables. If we are in need of nutritional assistance, we can seek advice from a professional nutritionist. If cost is a potential barrier, try contacting your local Area Agency on Aging (AOA). Local AOAs usually provide nutritional consulting on a sliding scale (for those caring for someone sixty years of age or older). We should try whatever works best for our circumstance to assist in eating well.

We should take time out for ourselves

We should schedule adequate time to do things that are important to us and make sure we keep interests outside our caregiving role. Knitting, reading, attending an exercise club, participating in a prayer group, or doing anything else outside caregiving is vitally important. When we practice taking time out for ourselves, it should not be something we would be required to do or learn as a part of our caregiver role. When we take a break, we should really take a break. We should not allow ourselves to get into the practice of spending all our time focusing on caregiving duties. We can ask ourselves about the last time we had time to get away, I mean truly get away, and have the opportunity to refresh, mind, body, and spirit. In our community, we offer an annual caregiver retreat. We try to make it a memorable experience for those attending. The theme of the retreat is "A Time for Me." Taking time for ourselves should be a daily practice, even if it is only a fifteen-minute walk. When we return to our duties, we will often be refreshed and revived; our spiritual baskets will be filled, our ideas will flow, and our true selves will have time in the sunlight. We should take the opportunity just to try it!

We should start our days properly

We should prepare the night before or have someone assist at night so we can get sleep during the evening. We can utilize respite services or whatever it takes to start our days with our best feet forward. We should allow adequate time for planning our days and schedule rest periods for ourselves. If we start our days properly, we will have the opportunity to handle most anything that comes our way.

We should not overfill our plates

There are things we have time to do and things we won't have time to do or don't want do. We shouldn't allow ourselves to feel pressured to do anything we do not want to do. This means not doing *anything* we do not want to do and not making excuses in doing so. I used to do this or that for the sake of not wanting to make another feel uncomfortable or disappointed. Then I would spend hours fretting over having to fulfill the commitment. Somehow, when doing things I didn't wish to do, I would end up disappointed in the end. We should practice the art of saying no, resist the temptation to overcommit, and watch the transformation. When I agree to do something, everyone understands the level of commitment a yes entails. When I decline an invitation or request, people generally understand.

We should plan quiet relaxation time

Take time to relax quietly without thinking or moving. We can just sit still and close our eyes to take our minds away from our present situations. Just sitting and not thinking, not doing, not talking can release us from our roles as husbands, wives, sons, daughters, brothers, sisters, nieces, or nephews. We are just relaxing.

We can calm ourselves quietly and inwardly when we are surrounded by chaos

We can use time to collect ourselves, taking deep, cleansing breaths as a way to relax and calm ourselves.

We should consider the following questions

What does this situation need? What can I bring to this situation? How can I help make the situation easier and/or build positive links for the future?

We should schedule time when the phone is off

I don't know if it's just me, but my phone seems to ring all the time, especially at times when I am in the middle of something very important. As soon as I begin a task or try to exercise or take a nap or a quiet bath, the phone rings. To avoid interruptions from the phone ringing, turn off the phone during quiet time. We can set the stage to clear our minds without interruptions. Callers will either leave a message or call back later.

We should avoid the trap of becoming addictive caregivers

Addictive caregiving relates to keeping ourselves in the cycle of caring for others and sparingly caring for ourselves. When we are addicted to caregiving, we are not stewards of personal growth.

When we take time to fill our spiritual needs and accomplish personal goals, we are able to live in harmony. When we are overworked, burned out, tired, and hungry, we may lack the harmony to maintain a positive outlook and be who we truly are.

We must recognize that if we do not take care of ourselves, no one else will. If we don't start taking care of ourselves, who will? If we don't take time to care for ourselves, when will it happen? Why shouldn't we start now? We can enjoy the practice of taking time away from our responsibilities to nurture our spirits and well-being.

Points to Ponder

1. What are some practices you can incorporate to fill your spiritual basket?

_____

_____

_____

_____

2. Is there anything you have not tried that you would like to try to care for yourself?

_____

_____

_____

_____

Famous Quote

May our Lord Jesus Christ himself and God our father who loved us and by his grace gave us eternal encouragement and good hope, encourage your hearts and strengthen you in every food deed and world.

—Thessalonians 2:16–17

TWENTY-TWO
Examining Our Attitudes

I wear my attitude on my sleeve,
and my heart is nearby,
each day's experiences help to shape feelings and
thoughts unselfishly hidden within my mind.
I wear my attitude on my sleeve,
and my heart is nearby,
each new day brings hope and a quest for happiness that
can't be purchased no matter what cost proposed.
I wear my attitude on my sleeve,
and my mind is nearby,
always thinking and planning ahead,
always in search of new experiences that will assist
with shaping new and exciting thoughts.
I wear my attitude on my sleeve,
and my heart is nearby,
each new day's experience helps me understand that my attitude
is reflected in my daily actions for everyone to see.
I wear my attitude on my sleeve,
and my heart is nearby,
to encourage a new approach that each new day affords an opportunity
to change my reactions and challenges the way I view others,
reminding me that I never have to change the way I truly feel.
I wear my attitude on my sleeve,
and my mind is nearby,
when I walk in the room everyone notices my self-
confidence, happiness and self-control.
For you must understand, my attitude is a very important part of me.

—Dr. Eboni Green

OUR ATTITUDE IS AN OUTWARD expression of how we are feeling
internally. Examining one's attitude takes wisdom and understanding.

121

The following story is a perfect display of being mindful of our attitude:

> An old Cherokee is teaching his grandson about life. "A fight is going on inside me," he says to the boy. "It is a terrible fight, and it is between two wolves. One is evil—he is anger, envy, sorrow, regret, greed, arrogance, self-pity, guilt, resentment, inferiority, lies, false pride, superiority, and ego. The other is good—he is joy, peace, love, hope, serenity, humility, kindness, benevolence, empathy, generosity, truth, compassion, and faith. The same fight is going on inside you, and inside every other person, too." The grandson thinks about it for a minute and then asks his grandfather, "Which wolf will win?" The old Cherokee simply replies, "The one you feed."

We must ask ourselves, which wolf we will feed? If we do not take time to feed the "good" wolf, the "evil" wolf will easily take control. The evil wolf represents our attitude, and the evil wolf is always hungry. If we do not allow the evil wolf to consume our thoughts and ideas, it will starve, dehydrate, and wither. On the other hand, if we are in the practice of feeding the evil wolf, the good wolf may become malnourished. When we allow others power over our emotions, we grant them control of our attitude. Positive or negative, attitude is reflected in everything we do in life.

The following are some suggestions to explore when examining one's attitude.

Recognize negative attitudes

Negative attitudes are like a cancer or a virus in that they spread quickly, and often, we only treat the symptoms. If there is someone who negatively affects our attitude, depresses us, and makes life unbearable, we should limit our interactions with him or her.

Practice making positive statements aloud

We do not have to wait for others to make positive statements about our level of commitment. We can give ourselves the gifts of forgiveness and self-preservation by appreciating what we are capable of, what we do to assist others, and the time we spend caring for ourselves. Additionally, we can praise ourselves for our accomplishments, no matter how minimal they may be to others. If we are waiting for others to offer praise, we may be waiting for a long time. Remember that whatever we do to assist our loved ones keeps them in the home and displays our love and commitment to caring. We can celebrate our successes by giving ourselves positive reinforcement and setting ourselves up for future successes.

Practice the art of offering and accepting positive feedback

On the continued path of spiritual and personal growth, we must get into the habit of giving and accepting positive feedback. Without understanding our strengths and weaknesses, we can never reach our highest level of spiritual functioning. Feedback gives us the legend, and commitment allows us to develop a road map for successful growth. When we offer constructive feedback to others, we give them the opportunity for self-improvement.

Discard negative statements

Have you ever conversed with someone and he or she immediately became defensive? It is in this pivotal moment that the conversation becomes counterproductive and communication is diminished. We can drop the subject and come back later, when open communication can truly occur.

Examine our general feelings toward life

We can examine how we feel when we wake up in the morning. What is our general feeling toward life? Do we have a positive or negative outlook? The way we start our morning spills over into the remainder of our day. Sometimes chaos is the name of the day from the moment we wake up. We have little control over many of the things that occur in life; however, we do have control over our perceptions and attitudes. We can greatly improve our success by starting off our day positively, waking up at a decent time, and eating a good breakfast. In addition, we can set time for solitude, quiet, and stillness to assist in keeping a positive attitude.

Say no and mean it

We cannot commit to doing everything everyone wants us to do. When we overcommit to meeting the expectations of others, frequently, the results do not meet our expectations. There have been many occasions when I was pressured to commit to something only to be disappointed by the outcome. My husband and I reluctantly made a trip of over five hundred miles to attend a wedding. The wedding party made plans for certain hotel accommodations. Because we were making such a long trip over a short weekend, we wanted to make it special, and to be honest, we didn't feel comfortable staying at the hotel in the area they selected. We ended up staying at a hotel fifteen minutes away from the wedding. We missed the wedding and spent hours trying to locate the rest of the family. We didn't see anyone for the remainder of the weekend. My husband and I had a wonderful time together, but we could have stayed in our hometown. We went out of obligation to meet the expectations of others. We should only agree to what we can and wish to do.

Try trading places

We do not have to physically exchange places with our loved ones; rather we can change places mentally. When someone we love has a different perspective, we can try listening first, and then try understanding. We should keep ourselves open to the perspectives of others.

Separate your view of yourself from the views of others

More often than not, we are not trying to change ourselves, but we attach our personal views to someone else's view of who we are, meaning that if someone negatively comments about our clothing or the way we apply our makeup, we immediately begin to self-evaluate. There are those offering truckloads of advice but are barely hanging on to life. We should not follow advice from those who surround themselves in negativity. Instead, we can allow ourselves to remember that every failure has the potential to become a success if we are learning in the process.

We do not have to change all at once; it has taken time to develop our thoughts, beliefs, and perspectives, and it will likewise take time to make changes we want to exhibit through actions.

Points to Ponder

1. What has this chapter taught you about the importance of attitude?

_____

_____

_____

_____

Famous Quote

Two men looked out through prison bars. The one saw mud the other stars.

—author unknown

TWENTY-THREE

Listening

Don't Tell Me That You Understand

Don't tell me that you understand,
Don't tell me that you know.
Don't tell me that I will survive,
How I will surely grow.
Don't tell me this is just a test,
That I am truly blessed,
That I am chosen for the task,
Apart from the rest.
Don't come at me with answers
That can only come from me,
Don't tell me how my grief will pass,
That I will soon be free.
Don't stand in pious judgment
Of the bonds I must untie,
Don't tell me how to grieve,
Don't tell me when to cry.
My life is filled with selfishness,
My pain is all I see,
But I need you and your love . . .
Unconditionally.
Accept me in my ups and downs,
I need someone to share.
Just hold my hand and let me cry,
And say, "My friend, I care."

—author unknown

DURING STRESSFUL TIMES, WE OFTEN wish someone would not only listen but also empathize with and ultimately understand our plight. Listening requires one to place preconceived ideas or notions to the side.

Although there may be portions of conversation with which we do not agree, we can gain insight and a better perspective if we only listen.

I recently received a telephone call from two of my best friends. They called to discuss the upcoming wedding of a mutual friend. As it turns out, I was the only bridesmaid yet to be fitted for my bridesmaid dress. The call was to prompt me to get fitted as soon as possible, as the wedding was just three weeks away. The timing for the call couldn't have been worse. I was mentally overwhelmed and equally stressed. I had so much on my plate already and was also planning my grandmother's memorial service. When I heard the two of them talking to me at the same time, I immediately became defensive. I started listing the reasons I had not been able to make the trip. As the conversation continued, I became enraged and started feeling as though my feelings were being minimized. I was talking about the loss of a grandparent, and they were talking about day-to-day stresses like child rearing and bills. I felt there was no comparison. So I yelled and cried, and they allowed me to do so. They gave me permission to vent, and they just listened. Once my feelings were validated, I realized I had made a promise, and I intended to keep it. I made it to the wedding, and I must say, I am glad I did—it was a beautiful wedding.

The only way we can truly listen is to keep an open mind, withholding judgment until we have all the facts. The following are two important types of listening when it comes to caregiving.

Listening to our inner voice

Our inner voice is our sixth sense, often suppressed in the part of the brain we know little about. It frequently warns us of impending situations, of danger, or of changes in the environment, especially when evidence is not necessarily tangible. Sometimes situations with our loved ones occur, and we have a gut feeling that something is just not right. This is the inner voice to which I am referring. We should grant ourselves permission to listen to what our inner voice is trying to relay and, if necessary, take action. Never has the importance of listening to my inner voice been as apparent as it was when my daughter was recently ill. When I took her to the emergency room, the doctors were dismissive of my concerns. She had a small rash all over her body and was suffering from excruciating headaches. I would not take no for an answer because I knew something was not right. The truth was she was having a severe allergic reaction to a prescription medication and ended up in the hospital for over a week. Whenever we think something is just not right with a loved one, we should persist until we get to the heart of the issue.

Listening without giving advice

Listening does not mean we agree. However, the longer we listen without interrupting, the more opportunities we have to understand the perspectives of others. Listening is an acquired skill that, once mastered, becomes an art form. Sometimes to really be there for someone, we must listen. We can allow ourselves to listen without giving advice, which is an important skill that will allow one to more fully appreciate the perspectives of others.

It is important for our loved ones to know that they can come to us and tell us how they feel. Talking things over will allow us to deepen our views and sometimes to broaden our perspectives. By listening, we encourage our loved ones to discuss circumstances completely. We can listen attentively without thinking of our countermove. When we actively listen, we attune ourselves to the desires and needs of others. Undivided attention in and of itself nurtures, comforts, and encourages people. We can find that quiet place inside, that place that allows us a reprieve to become better listeners.

Points to Ponder

1. Try listening without making any judgments. Write down any thoughts you have after the experience.

_____

_____

_____

_____

2. What changes do you see when you take the approach of listening, instead of always talking?

_____

_____

_____

_____

3. Are there any examples where listening to your inner voice was effective in letting you know there was something wrong with your loved one?

_____

_____

_____

_____

Famous Quote

Salt is good but if it loses its saltiness, there is no way to make it salty again. It is no good for the soil or for the manure pile; it is thrown away. Listen if you have ears.

—Luke 14:3

TWENTY-FOUR

Keeping Things Simple

The human spirit, flexible in nature, open to new ideas, free from ridged
expectations . . . for the human spirit represents the essence of an individual.
The simplistic soul exudes freedom, versatility and
ultimately triumphs over the adversities life presents.
The human spirit is never callus nor does it act in uncaring
ways for it has no choice but to listen to the expressions
of the soul, always spoken in frank terms.
The true, simplistic human spirit is forgiving, humble and
uncompounded. Tirelessly treating others as complete or whole,
through actions expressing nothing less than compassion.
This practice is natural for the simplistic soul, for it has no
choice but to transcend, transfigure and transform.
All effortless for the soul dedicated to the path of simplicity.

—Dr. Eboni Green

THROUGH THE ENDLESS COMPLEXITIES LIFE presents, we must commit
to taking a more simplistic approach if we seek longevity in our
caregiving. The practice of simplicity accounts for the need to rid
ourselves of unnecessary expectations, especially unrealistic goals we
set for ourselves. The practice of simplicity takes into account noticing,
appreciating, and understanding our individual journeys, including
all the bumps in the road. More importantly, keeping things simple
means staying grounded for future challenges because we know they
are coming. When the practice of simplicity is omitted, for all intents
and purposes, areas in life are bound to have shortcomings.

The following is a list of possible pitfalls to avoid on the path to
simplifying our present circumstances.

Overbooking

We should not keep our schedules booked without the need for overbooking, not setting time between tasks as well as taking on too many roles, thus leaving little or no time for ourselves.

Keeping focus on present situations

We should not allow ourselves to get stuck focusing on problems in present situations. Instead, we can try opening our minds to the possibilities. None of our approaches have to be permanent; we can try, try, and try again.

Telling ourselves what can't be or won't be accomplished

We should try not to set limits on what we can do for ourselves; instead, we can use a collective approach. If we work together, there is almost nothing we cannot accomplish. Instead of telling ourselves what can't be done, we should focus on what can be done to change or improve our circumstances.

Enjoying where we are

We may be focusing on when things get better or when they will be different. Why not focus on the small successes we have daily? We shouldn't sit around waiting for life to happen. Remember that life is happening right now—it's how we perceive our lives that makes all the difference. We should try to enjoy where we are, right now, today!

When we place the practice of simplicity on hold, other areas in life are bound to have shortcomings. However, when we open ourselves to keeping things simple, we increase our opportunities for positive and long-lasting results.

Points to Ponder

1. What are some ways the practice of simplicity can be incorporated into your life?

_____

_____

_____

_____

2. Are there things that can be delegated to increase your chances of having a more simplistic approach to life?

_____

_____

_____

_____

3. Is there anything holding you back? If so, what is it, and is there anything you can do to remove or decrease obstacles?

_____

_____

_____

_____

Famous Quote

All man's busy rushing ends in nothing. He heaps up riches for someone else to spend. On a deathbed, no one ever laments, "I wish I had spent more time at the office."

—author unknown

TWENTY-FIVE
Change Begins in the Heart

Anything brittle breaks when bent; unless you
want to crumble, stay flexible.

—Dr. Eboni Green

CHANGE BEGINS IN THE HEART but cannot happen without cooperation between the heart and the mind. When we are learning, we begin by absorbing new information. It is through experiences that we are given life education to begin making changes in our lives, and the more we learn, the more we realize we don't know. No matter how hard we try, we cannot change anyone except ourselves. As caregivers, we want to make small and gradual personal changes that will in turn alter our relationships and motivate us to continue moving forward.

Inflexibility has led to many problems in our homes, communities, and the world in general. When we enter situations with preconceived ideas, our ability to remain flexible is hindered. The practice of being flexible will propel us to reach our goals and bounce back from challenges with resiliency. To stay flexible, we must understand our need for continued growth. If we come to terms with the fact that we don't know everything, then we understand that flexibility will enable opportunities to glean additional information from those in our inner circles.

Test Your Flexibility

	Frequently	Sometimes	Never
I am open to the suggestions of others.	3	2	1
I focus my attention on elevating the self-esteem of others.	3	2	1
I can see different points of view.	3	2	1
I am tolerant and willing to accommodate others.	3	2	1
I exhibit my commitment to change through my actions.	3	2	1
I am willing to try as many approaches to a problem as necessary.	3	2	1
When an approach is ineffective, I am willing to try a new approach.	3	2	1
Others would say I am flexible.	3	2	1
I give those in my inner circle permission to do the right thing.	3	2	1

Total Score_____

- If your score is 23 to 27, you are open to change.
- If your score is 23 to 18, you are fairly flexible.
- If your score is 17 to 9, you should consider working on your flexibility.

The practice of flexibility can open doors to allow us to let go. We can practice letting go by releasing past, present, and thoughts of future challenges that would inhibit personal growth. We can think of a suitcase on a baggage carousel going around and around until someone claims it or it is retrieved by the attendant. If no one claims the suitcase, attendants have little choice but to retain unclaimed baggage. When we hold on to unresolved issues and push feelings down into hidden places, we become baggage attendants for someone else's baggage. We must understand that people are prone to mistakes and leave their problems on the baggage carousel. We shouldn't try to pick them up, or else we may wake up one day to find ourselves bogged down by the problems and baggage of others.

We should allow ourselves flexibility, keeping in mind that much of what we do daily has never been done before. Each day we care, we are authoring our personal all-inclusive handbook. We can remind ourselves daily of the importance of the job we do. We can also learn to appreciate our resourcefulness and ability to use creative approaches to address problems as they arise.

We should maintain flexibility with ourselves. We can't expect others to be flexible if we do not practice forgiveness. Flexibility with others frees brain and heart capacity. With freed brains and hearts, our spirits and the spirits of our loved ones will be uplifted. Uplifted spirits and renewed hearts can give us the strength to continue caring. We can allow ourselves to fully explore opportunities life has to offer through flexibility. Remember that change begins in the heart!

Points to Ponder

1. What have you learned about your flexibility?

_____

_____

_____

_____

2. Try listing ways to become more flexible.

_____

_____

_____

_____

Famous Quote

It is a great challenge this path of the householder. There are many distractions, many worldly.

—Neale Donald Walsch[45]

TWENTY-SIX

Loving One Another as We Love Ourselves

I may be able to speak the languages of men and even of angels,
but if I have no love, my speech is no more than
a noisy gong or a clanging bell.
I may have all knowledge and understand all secrets; I may have all the
faith needed to move mountains—but if I have no love, I am nothing.
I may give away everything I have, and even give up my body
to be burned—but if I have no love, this does me no good.
Love is patient and kind; it is not jealous or conceited or proud;
love is not ill mannered or selfish or irritable; love does not keep a record
of wrongs; love is not happy with evil, but is happy with the truth.
Love never gives up; and its faith, hope, and patience never fail.
Love is eternal.

—1 Corinthians 13:1–8

LOVE IS THE SOIL IN which we grow; the sunlight determines the direction, and the water nourishes our growth. No matter our age, we never outgrow the need or desire for love. We do not outgrow love because the power of love is exponential. Closeness and warmth coupled with love are essential to human growth and development.

The practice of touch is often used in neonatal units and for the terminally ill. Through the power of touch, we allow ourselves to offer some degree of affection, appreciation, and acceptance to others. Everyday acts of kindness are what make life worth living; we only hope that we are able to grant this gift to others and that others will bestow the same gift on us.

Growing up, I remember reciting the golden rule: "Do unto others as you would have them do unto you." Although I agree, I think that "loving one another as we love ourselves" has a little more weight. Even when we have inner conflict, we love ourselves. As caregivers, this means loving others and understanding them so that we may care for them in the best possible way. Love can be defined as a strong personal attachment, strong liking or fondness, or devotion to another. Love comes from the heart and is expressed through compassion displayed in interactions with others. Love is about actions, awareness, and interconnection with our inward beings.

We should keep love in our hearts and minds while we care for those in our inner circles, but more important, we shouldn't forget to love ourselves.

Points to Ponder

1. Try listing five things you love about yourself.

   _____

   _____

   _____

   _____

2. Try listing five things you love about your loved one.

   _____

   _____

   _____

   _____

Keep your list in a place where you can review it. Your list can act as a reminder of the great attributes you possess.

Famous Quote

The mountains and hills may crumble, but my love for you will never end; I will keep forever my promise of peace.

—Isaiah 54:10

TWENTY-SEVEN
Roadblocks

A boy found an eagle's egg and he put it in the nest of a prairie chicken. The eagle hatched and thought he was a chicken. He grew up doing what prairie chickens do—scratching at the dirt for food and flying short distances with a noisy fluttering of wings. It was a dreary life. Gradually the eagle grew old and bitter. One day he and his prairie chicken friend saw a beautiful bird soaring on the currents of air, high above the mountains. "Oh, I wish I could fly like that!" said the eagle. The chicken replied, "Don't give it another thought. That's the mighty eagle, the king of all birds—you could never be like him!" And the eagle didn't give it another thought. He went on cackling and complaining about life. He died thinking he was intended to be an eagle, so don't listen to the prairie chicken! Recognize him for what he is: a road block.

—author unknown

THERE CAN BE NUMEROUS ROADBLOCKS and dips in the road when we are caring for a sick or disabled loved one. Roadblocks of life are frequently manifested in two different ways: through people and circumstances.

People are frequently roadblocks because of their placing self-interests over the need to support the greater good. Now, there is nothing wrong with having some level of self-interest—our personal interests serve useful purposes such as staying motivated or finding our calling in life. We wouldn't take time to do some of the things we do if we didn't have just the smallest bit of self-interest.

However, when self-interest precludes everything or becomes the catalyst for every decision, there is something seriously wrong. This is the "what's in it for me" mentality. We wonder, what am I going to get out of anything I do? Both these questions have the word *me* or *I* in them. While there are times when reciprocation is necessary, the times when it is not necessary are far more numerous.

Sometimes it is more difficult to move around the person blocking the road. The more intent we are, the more intent such a person becomes on standing in our way. The only way to counteract counterproductive people is to face them and move on. We should stop them in their tracks and firmly express our knowledge of their intentions and actions.

We should not allow others to hinder our attainment of personal goals or force us to stumble. We should give ourselves freedom to explore who we really are. Understand that stumbling blocks are called "stumbling blocks" for a reason: in most cases, we are going to stumble. If we stumble, we are slowed down momentarily; however, once we get past the hindrance, it becomes a thing of the past.

If circumstances are blocking our progress, we should take a step back and take a moment to assess the situation. We should really look at what is occurring in our lives and our part in making things the way they are. We can take time to make mental adjustments and evaluate our current approaches to how we presently accomplish diverting blocks in the road. Are we getting the desired results? If the answer is yes, then wonderful, and congratulations. However, some of us get in ruts, and there may be changes made in our approaches and interactions to circumvent roadblocks.

The good news is that once we identify what is blocking our progress and make adjustments, we can continue moving right along and work toward regaining our momentum.

Points to Ponder

1. What can you do to make sure others do not hinder your progress?

_____

_____

_____

_____

2. Try listing times when you have stumbled. What did you learn from the experience?

_____

_____

_____

_____

3. Have you ever been a stumbling block to someone? Is there something you can do to ensure you are not someone else's stumbling block?

_____

_____

_____

_____

Famous Quote

The worst mistake you can make is to give up on yourself and stop challenging yourself for fear of failure. Keep moving forward with a firm eye on the future, telling yourself, "I'll start from today!" "I'll start afresh from now, from this very moment!"

—Daisaku Ikeda

TWENTY-EIGHT

Exploring a Healthy Spirituality: Our Personal Relationship with God

Spiritual Affirmation

God represents life,
both spiritual and natural,
and He is housed in my heart.
He knows my heart and soul desires better than I.
God is the only power that can control life, spirit, body and mind.
I am a representation of God's love just as I am today.
He does not make mistakes, people do, but it is how we learn
and grow from our mistakes that brings us closer to Him.

—Dr. Eboni Green

SPIRITUALITY DOES NOT NECESSARILY RELATE to religious activities or rituals; rather, spirituality defines the act of adding meaning to our lives and the lives of those for whom we care.

The very word *spirituality* has multitudinous meanings and definitions. Simply put, spirituality is an individual relationship with God, different from any other relationship. Spirituality is an inner search for meaning or fulfillment that may be undertaken by anyone. True spiritual practice is a marriage of the mind, body, and spirit.

Perceptions may be that if by all outward appearances, a person looks to be enjoying life, he or she must be healthy spiritually. In all actuality, each of us experiences difficult, trying, and stressful times. Additionally, we may experience feelings of guilt associated with the inability to meet personal spiritual needs. Sometimes we may even feel alone. The truth of the matter is that with a strong spiritual base, we are never alone.

When we choose to take a proactive approach to spiritual nourishment, we open ourselves to the full experience of caring for another. A proactive caregiver views his or her cup as half full, understanding that no matter where he or she is going, the journey is what matters most. The practice of being spiritually proactive begins when we give ourselves permission to separate *being* from *doing*. If we are always *doing*, when will there be time to exhibit gifts of patience and stillness? In separating *being* and *doing*, we increase our opportunities to express who we really are. In truth, we are so much more than what we do to provide service to others. We should not allow ourselves to become accustomed to always doing something physical; instead, we can take a moment out of each hour to relax and just *be*. Some of my most productive times have been when I haven't had anything to do. Silence can be one of our greatest gifts to assist us in growing. Cultivating spirituality can have positive implications, adding to the caring experience. It is through positive caring experiences that the hunger for spiritual transformation often becomes apparent.

Spiritual transformation allows one to evolve into a complete being, offering at a minimum some level of completeness to our caregiving journey. By separating *being* from *doing*, we allow ourselves time for nurturing to make the most out of every day.

Sometimes we place our personal and spiritual needs on the back burner and market ourselves to meet the needs of others. Even if we are not planning to have a half-empty cup, when we ignore our personal needs, our cup drips, losing its ability to become full, thus opening the door to stress. Spiritual stress often leads to spiritual distress. Spiritual distress can cause a person to question his or her value system and, in general, the meaning of life. We may feel or say that we no longer have a reason to live. Jack Wintz[46] reminded us that "what God is all about is not inflicting blindness or cancer or earthquakes upon people, but just the opposite. The removal of such scourges. God's Glory is revealed in healing these evils." When sickness occurs, our faith can be tested, and we may question our relationship with God.

Growing toward Spiritual Equals in a Caregiving Partnership

Care Receiver Spiritual Hierarchy (Burdened Caregiver)	Care Receiver/ Caregiver Spiritual Opposition (Burdened Caregiver/ Burdened Care Receiver)	Care Receiver/Caregiver Spiritual Equality (Spiritual Equality)
The personal needs of the care receiver take precedence over the emotional, physical, and spiritual needs of the caregiver.	Personal needs of the caregiver/ care receiver are fully recognized, although they may not be equally met (caregiver needs to have respite, caregiver support, housekeeper, companion, or other services).	Personal needs of the caregiver and the care receiver are equally respected.
Care receiver accepts little or no responsibility for meeting his or her personal needs.	Care receiver attempts to accept responsibility for personal care as a partner.	Caregiver and care receivers are partners in meeting one another's needs, taking a team approach.
Care receiver accepts as much as possible from the caregiver to decrease his or her personal responsibility.	Care receiver attempts to accept responsibility from the caregiver to decrease his or her personal responsibilities through guilt.	Care receiver understands and accepts that the two are a team. Decreased burden and guilt by making it easier for the caregiver to accept help without guilt.
Caregiver would not think of asking for assistance. "I can manage myself."	Caregiver is hesitant to say no to the demands of the care receiver.	Caregiver gives self permission to say no, but only when there is a genuine need to say no.
Caregiver becomes exhausted and drained emotionally, loses his or her sense of self, and loses touch with his or her personal ability to be a productive caregiver.	Caregiver becomes exhausted and "contemplates" his or her worth as a caregiver. May question, is it worth it all? Would like to accept respite but feels too guilty and resentful.	Caregiver/care receiver become expressive and open to creativity and plan for future needs. Open communication between the caregiver and care receiver increases, and spirituality blossoms.

Longevity as a caregiver lies in our ability to rely on a sound spiritual base. When we improperly care for ourselves, it can equate to self-inflicted abuse. When we ignore our personal and physical needs, in essence, our capacity to care for another suffers. To the contrary, in giving ourselves permission to take into account our personal needs and nurture ourselves, our caregiving capacity soars.

By shifting our spiritual hierarchy system completely, we honor the role of "caregiver" as a worthy calling. We can encourage ourselves to plant our feet and spiritual needs solidly, separate from our caregiving duties. Additionally, we can recognize ourselves as whole, worthy spiritual beings. These practices will make it easier, bit by bit, to feel strong enough and safe enough emotionally to express original creative ideas and to ask for whatever we need to perform our role as caregivers. We can maximize our capacity and concentrate on our true roles in life. Individually, our hearts determine our destined purpose. Remember that we are mapping our appropriate journeys. We should recognize the epiphany, awakening as it occurs through the compassion expressed, through our mission to serve through caring.

Points to Ponder

1. What, if anything, is keeping you from being complete in your role to care for and about others?

_____

_____

_____

_____

2. Could your personal relationship with God be a motivating factor for caring?

_____

_____

_____

_____

Famous Quote

A study of 92,000 Maryland residents found church attendance significantly associated with reduced morbidity and mortality.

—Comstock and Partridge[47]

Epilogue:
The Summer of Life

We often hear about the winter of life, when the days are short and the
trees are bare without leaves and there are only branches left to see.
But what about the summer of life, when spring has already passed and
fall and winter have not yet approached. There is the summer of life.
The summer of life brings with it long days, where the
sun shines freely in its splendid exuberance.
The summer of life brings with it bountiful benefits
that we will reap with the fall harvest.
Reflections of summer are what we review, remember and cherish during
the long winter months when we forget what the sun has to offer.
The summer of life lends a baseline and endures for memory's sake.
The summer flies by rapidly when it seems as
though the summer has only just begun.
During the summer, everything is in full bloom, but when the sunshine
disappears in the winter, we lack the nurturing warmth of the summer.
Without the occasional soft summer rain, our grass and flowers
wilt and turn brown in the blistering summer sun.
The summer of life brings a medley of tastes and an array of
colors. In the summer everything seems bright, noticeable,
and all God's creatures come out to enjoy the earth.
Without fond reflections of the radiant earth, we
cannot sustain the winter cabin fever.
Colorless winters of life, times for reflection of past summer vacations,
are present to remember, and the experiences are there to draw upon.
The summer of life strengthens, sustains and holds us together.
So you see, summer can be more important than winter; the
memories of the summer of life last an entire lifetime.

—Dr. Eboni Green

AT THE BEGINNING OF OUR spiritual journey, we prayed to find out what it all means. The meaning of caring as well as the meaning of life for me came in a moment of clarity. It means being there for someone simply because we care. It means exhibiting patience and understanding. It means taking in all life has to offer and making every day worth living. It means continuing to grow while we learn to care for and about ourselves with the utmost sincerity for continued growth.

Let us end with a prayer

I pray that we honor our lives by living each day independently of all others, by keeping an open mind, and by understanding that anything is possible. I pray we don't set limits on what we can do and that we don't bank on things occurring the way they are planned. I pray to understand the many challenges we will face. I pray for the wisdom, understanding, and patience to cope with the outcomes, come what may. *I pray that we live every day like the summer of life and that our spiritual journey is a journey well traveled. Amen!*

Notes

Foreword

1. Bob Deits, *Life after Loss: A Practical Guide to Renewing Your Life after Experiencing Major Loss* (Cambridge: Lifelong Books, 2004), 34.

2. Lance Armstrong, "Lance Armstrong (1971–)," http://www.lancearmstrong.com/.

3. John Vance Cheney, *Complete Poems of John V Chencey* (Cambridge: Riverside Press, 1906), 87.

4. John Henry Jowett, *The Silver Lining* (New York: Grosset and Dunlap, 1907), 192.

5. Edwin Hubble Chapin as reported in Josiah Hotchkess Gilbert, *Dictionary of Burning Words of Brilliant Writers* (New York: W. B. Ketcham, 1895).

6. Jack Wintz, *Making Sense out of Suffering* (Meinrad, IN: Abby Press, 1996).

Introduction

7. Henri J. M. Nouwen, *Reaching Out: The Three Movements of the Spiritual Life* (New York: Doubleday, 1966).

8. Black History Pages, "Octavia E. Butler (1947–2006)," http://www.blackhistorypages.net/pages/obutler.php.

9. *Merriam-Webster's Collegiate Dictionary*, 15th ed., s.v. "Journey."

10. Stephen R. Covey, *Principle-Centered Leadership* (New York: Fireside, 1990), 17.

11. James E. Miller, *What Will Help Me? 12 Things to Remember When You Have Suffered a Loss* (Fort Wayne, IN: WillowGreen, 2000),

One

12. Dough Toft, Mel Pohl, and Deniston Kay, *The Caregiver's Journey: When You Love Someone with AIDS* (New York: HarperCollins, 1999).

13. Douglas Pagels, *The Language of Courage and Inner Strength: A Wonderful Gift of Inspiring Thoughts* (Boulder, CO: SPS Studios, 1999), 7.

Two

14. Richard Carlson, *Don't Sweat the Small Stuff* (New York: Hyperion, 1997), 86.

15. Douglas Pagels, *The Language of Courage and Inner Strength: A Wonderful Gift of Inspiring Thoughts* (Boulder, CO: SPS Studios, 1999), 1.

Three

16. *Merriam-Webster's Collegiate Dictionary*, 15th ed., s.v. "Faith."

17. Bruce Bickel and Stan Jantz, *God Is in the Tough Stuff* (Uhrichville, OH: Barbour, 2005), 14.

18. Abraham H. Maslow, "A Theory of Human Motivation," *Psychological Review* 50 (1943): 370–96.

19. C. S. Lewis, *Letters to an American Lady,* http://www.lewissociety.org/quotes.php.

20. Quoted in Zig Ziglar, *Confessions of a Grieving Christian* (Nashville, TN: B&H, 2004), 77.

21. New Hope, "Robert H. Schuller (1926–)," http://www.newhopenow.org/schuller/tragedy/sermon_36.html.

22. Good Reads, "St. Francis de Sales (1567–1622)," http://www.goodreads.com/author/quotes/226264.St_Francis_de_Sales.

Five

23. Doe Lang, *The New Secrets of Charisma: How to Discover and Unleash Your Hidden Powers* (Lincolnwood, IL: Contemporary Books, 1999).

Six

24. Linda Hischhorn, "Writing Sermons," http://www.lindahischhorn.com/writings/al_khet.html.

Eight

25. Taro Gold, *Open Your Mind, Open Your Life: A Little Book of Eastern Wisdom* (Kansas City: Lionstead, 2001), 13.

Twelve

26. Steven Covey, *Seven Habits of Highly Effective People* (New York: Free Press, 1990), 289.

27. Garry Hamel and C.K. Prahalad, *Competing for the Future* (Boston: Harvard Press, 1994).

28. Iyanla Vanzant, *One Day My Soul Just Opened Up: 40 Days and Nights toward Spiritual Strength and Personal Growth* (New York: Simon and Schuster, 1999), 9.

Thirteen

29. Tolbert McCarroll, *The Tao, Sacred Way* (New York: Crossroad, 1982), 43.

30. Richard Carlson, *Don't Sweat the Small Stuff* (New York: Hyperion, 1997), 21.

31. Vince Lombardi, "Vince Lombardi Quotes," http://www.quotes-motivationl.com/motivational/vincelombari-quotes.html.

32. Dr. Phil (1950–), http://www.drphil.com/.

Fourteen

33. Rachel Harris and Dorothy Law Nolte, *Children Learn What They Live: Parenting to Inspire Values* (New York: Workman, 1998), 37.

34. Marcrina Wiederkehr, *Seasons of Your Heart:: Prayers and Reflections* (New York: HarperCollins, 1991), XX.

Sixteen

35. Taro Gold, *Open Your Mind, Open Your Life: A Little Book of Eastern Wisdom* (Kansas City: Lionstead, 2001), 9.

Seventeen

36. Dale Carnegie, *How to Win Friends and Influence People* (New York: Pocket Books, 1990), 17.

37. Roy P. Basler, *Collected Works of Abraham Lincoln*, Abraham Lincoln Association, http://quod.lib.umich.edu/Lincoln/.

Nineteen

38. Edwin Hubble Chapin, *Living Words* (Charleston, SC: Bibliolife, 2009), 185.

39. Leon Bloy, 1846–1917.

Twenty

40. Dr. Phil (1950–), http://www.drphil.com/.

41. Richard Carlson, *Don't Sweat the Small Stuff* (New York: Hyperion, 1997), 8.

42. Dale Carnegie, *How to Win Friends and Influence People* (New York: Pocket Books, 1990), 145.

43. Ibid., 7.

44. Ibid., 50.

Twenty-five

45. Neale Donald Walsch, *Conversations with God* (New York: Puttman Adult, 1996), 46.

46. Jack Wintz, *Making Sense out of Suffering* (Meinrad, IN: Abby Press, 1996).

47. G. W. Comstock and K. B. Partridge, "Church Attendance and Health," *Journal of Chronic Diseases* 25 (1972): 665–72.

About the Author

Dr. Eboni Green has extensive experience focused on training, assessing, and supporting front-line direct caregivers, with an emphasis in caregiver stress, burnout, and related family conflicts. She is an educator and published author on family caregiving and cofounded Caregiver Support Services with her husband.

Caregiver Support Services

Caregiver Support Services is a grassroots nonprofit organization with a 501(c)(3) tax-exempt status. The organization was founded by Terrence and Eboni Green, a husband and wife team, to support family & professional caregivers across the lifespan through direct supportive services. Caregiver Support Services is known nationally for creating benchmark programs and services for family and professional caregivers in the form of offering accessible training, self-advocacy, and other support services to assist caregivers through the care process.

For more information about our services please visit our Web site at http://www.caregiversupportservices.org.

ALSO BY DR. EBONI IVORY GREEN

Caregiving in the New Millennium